Through Much Tribulation

Gerhard Stuewe

World rights reserved. This book or any portion thereof may not be copied or reproduced in any form or manner whatever, except as provided by law, without the written permission of the publisher, except by a reviewer who may quote brief passages in a review.

The author assumes full responsibility for the accuracy of all facts and quotations as cited in this book. The opinions expressed in this book are the author's personal views and interpretations, and do not necessarily reflect those of the publisher.

This book is provided with the understanding that the publisher is not engaged in giving spiritual, legal, medical, or other professional advice. If authoritative advice is needed, the reader should seek the counsel of a competent professional.

Copyright © 2014 Gerhard Stuewe
Copyright © 2014 TEACH Services, Inc.
ISBN-13: 978-1-4796-0402-9 (Paperback)
ISBN-13: 978-1-4796-0403-6 (ePub)
ISBN-13: 978-1-4796-0404-3 (Mobi)
Library of Congress Control Number: 2014948851

All scripture quotations are taken from the King James Version. Public domain.

Published by

www.TEACHServices.com • (800) 367-1844

"We must through much tribulation enter into the kingdom of God." Acts 14:22

The following story is one of God's providential care and marvelous guidance in the life of our family, in peaceful days as well as amid the turmoil and hostility of war.

Dedication

This book is dedicated to the memory of my loving parents, Paul Ernst and Martha Stüwe, and to the memory of my sisters, Lotte Grunst, Lieschen Draheim, and Irmgard Volkmann. But also to my sister Renate Stüwe, as well as to my own family in the firm hope that they will remain faithful to Him who saves to the uttermost.

A special thanks goes to my favorite sister, Irmgard, who helped to refresh the youthful impressions I have of those horrible war years with her vivid memory.

Also, I wish to express my gratitude to the staff of TEACH Services, for the invaluable and much-appreciated help I received from them.

Introduction

All afternoon the storm clouds had been gathering on the eastern horizon. At first they looked like harmless, little white lambs, floating in an endless pasture of azure above the peaceful countryside of our native Pomerania/Germany. But that changed rather soon. Now they appeared to grow and change quickly, resembling grotesque wild horsemen on charging mounts, racing across an angry black sky.

The old farmstead crouched, as it were, behind the mighty trees that almost surrounded it, ready to weather another storm like all the others it had survived before in its many centuries of existence. However, this one was totally different from all the others it had withstood so far. Never before had the brutal forces gathered with such a fury and mighty show of primeval power. The branches of the old trees heaved and swayed wildly to the fearful scream of the infernal storm. All that were brittle, weak, or dead broke off and came down with a terrifying crash.

At the windswept corner of the thatch roof, post-and-beam barn, a small flock of sparrows busily fed on grain scattered on the ground. Last year's harvest had been good. God had abundantly blessed the fields, and kind hearts had not forgotten the little birds that lived about the farmstead. Presently, their lively chirping was almost swallowed up by the howling noise of the storm.

While all their attention was directed toward the search for food, suddenly a sparrow hawk swooped across the farmyard. On skilled wings he zoomed over the lilac bush that grew beside the barn, which he so masterfully used to conceal his stealthy approach, and pounced down on the unsuspecting birds. His sharp talons pierced a hapless little bird and locked instantly on its prey so that the sparrow had no chance to escape. Then, as sudden as the hawk had come, it disappeared again in the brewing darkness of the storm with the small sparrow hanging from its talons.

At the very moment the sparrow hawk showed up, the flock of sparrows scrambled in mad confusion in all directions. Only a few ruby-colored droplets of blood in the farmyard dirt testified of the drama, the struggle of life and death, that had just unfolded and which we too share with all of God's creatures, large and small, ever since the fall of Adam and Eve.

However, not long afterward, hesitantly at first, one by one the little sparrows came back again, soon happily chirping as before, looking for the bits of oat and rye that sustained their lowly lives. And yes, a long, long time after that terrible storm had passed, the sun once again shone on the small flock of sparrows.

The storm that I have briefly described here was none other than the Second World War, and the family of sparrows represents my family who, thanks to God's providence and guidance, weathered the horrors of war. Kindled by the insane passions of revengeful, power-hungry madmen, World War II resulted in the destruction of the lives and homes of millions of innocent human beings in many different parts of the world. One of the places that was destroyed was Pomerania, an eastern province of the former German Reich situated on the shores of the Baltic Sea. Pomerania was our home. For centuries our family and kinfolk had lived a peaceful and unassuming life in this beautiful countryside until the day that we, just like the little sparrows, fled the terror of war, but unlike the sparrows we would never return again.

Even though much of this story is about the hardship, fears, anxiety, and tribulation our family experienced while trying to escape the gruesome atrocities of that war, it is also about the providence of a loving heavenly Father who guided us in those perilous days.

Chapter 1

Before I tell you about the war, let me share some of the sunnier days of our lives in faraway Pomerania. My great-great grandparents on my father's side, Johann and Philiplepine Stüwe, were humble peasants on the estate of Alt-Reblin, about ten kilometers west of the town of Stolp. Our ancestors have lived in this little village since the end of the 1700s. In all likelihood, they settled there much earlier, but since all written records, which were usually kept by the clergy in the country churches, have been destroyed in the many wars that were fought in the past centuries on Pomeranian soil, nothing concrete is known about anything before the end of the 1700s. My great-grandfather Herrman, as well as my grandfather Karl Heinrich were born in this same village.

The estate owner, a man of old Pomeranian nobility, was a Freemason, and my Dad used to tell us a story about an incident that happened to my great-grandparents that "made your blood run cold," to use a phrase from poet Robert Service of Yukon fame. But before I continue with that story, let me first enlighten you a little about the peasant life on the estate. Granted, this information came to me secondhand, so to speak, but I know that neither my parents, nor my in-laws, had any interest in exaggerating their own or their parents' hardships in any way. (No, dear reader, it is not true that life was better in the good old days as some people claim. I thank God that I did not have to live in those "good old days.")

The peasants of Pomerania, or for that matter, the world over, had more than just a hard life to contend with. Generally, their lot was so bad that they barely made a living, even though they worked hard from early morning till late at night. Since they, for all practical purposes, belonged to the estate, like the cattle, sheep, and pigs, it depended completely on the estate owner how they fared. If he was a God-fearing man, they might have it a little better; otherwise, theirs was a life of unspeakable toil and hardship at best.

Since medieval times all land was owned by the nobility. Small parcels were leased to the peasants at exorbitant fees that most of them were unable to meet. Most peasants had to work the better part of every week for the landowners, so they were unable to properly care for their own fields. This, combined with the inferior agricultural practices of those days, resulted in poor crops. Poorer crops resulted in less money to pay the taxes. And if the peasant was unable to pay his lease, he was simply thrown off the property with no place to go except to another estate. It was one big, vicious circle.

In the days when my ancestors worked for the estate owner in Alt-Reblin, the system had changed somewhat. They did not lease land from the estate. Instead, they were day laborers who lived on the estate. Nevertheless, a desire for a better life stared from their inexpressive faces and peeped out of every nook and cranny of their impoverished abodes, which, by the way, also belonged to the estate. To help improve their dire conditions a bit, they were allowed to keep a cow or pig, some chickens and geese, as well as a potato patch. The meager wages for their hard labor were largely paid in the form of things like produce and cereals.

A day laborer's hovel, or cottage as it is properly called in English, was usually constructed of oak posts and beams. The space between the posts and beams was generally filled with wattle and daub and after 1800 with kiln-baked bricks. The roof was built of beams and covered with a thick layer of thatch, which was reed or rye straw. If the thatch was properly installed and maintained, it would last a lifetime and longer. Most of these dwellings had chimneys; however, older ones did not and were thus called smoke houses.

If you thought a smoking, smoldering campfire was bad for your eyes and lungs when the wind was blowing toward you, imagine living in a hovel without a chimney? Both my mother and mother-in-law spent their childhood in such smoke houses and related to me what it was like to live in such a place. When the wind prevented the smoke from escaping through the smoke holes in the roof or gables, they had to crawl on hands and knees on the floor, gasping for the little bit of oxygen that was near the floor, coughing and wiping tears from their eyes. I must confess that I like a fireplace in the house, but I would not want to have one without a chimney!

Windows were few and rather small, and if a windowpane happened to break, it was generally replaced with cardboard, paper, or even old rags since there was not always enough money for a new glass pane. Most often there was only a front entrance to the dwelling. This door would sometimes be of a Dutch-style design, like a barn door. By opening only the upper portion of the door, the animals, like geese and calves, could be kept outside, yet fresh air could enter freely.

Upon entering the dwelling, there was a narrow hallway. The floor was usually paved with flat fieldstones. All other floors in the house were generally of tamped clay or loam. From the hallway one came into the *stube*, the combined living room/kitchen. Here, facing the hallway, was the hearth, built of red bricks, on which all the cooking was done. On the back wall of the room stood the huge *Kachelofen*, the ceramic tiled heating stove that often had a narrow seat on one side which came in handy after a long, hard day working outside in the fall and particularly the winter. The heating stoves were often made of squared fieldstones, which were cheaper to obtain. The stove had in its foundation a spacious *Hölle*, "hell" as it was called, a place for the ashes. After the fire had gone out, this "hell" would sometimes double as an emergency nursery for sickly piglets and other small creatures like chicks and goslings that were in need of a warm place.

Beside the large living room/kitchen there was often a small bedchamber. The bedsteads were filled with straw in which fleas, bedbugs, lice, and mice set up residence. The larger cousins of the mice, the Norwegian rats, claimed, if allowed, the entire dwelling as their domain. To keep these uninvited guests at tolerable levels, one kept good cats in the home as well.

On account of the post-and-beam and wattle-and-daub construction, the walls of these dwellings were, except for the warmer, drier summer months, quite moist. Therefore, they were usually covered with a thick, moldy layer of fungus. In wintertime ice crystals glittered on the walls and the wind would whistle and chill the home as it blew through the many cracks in the windows, doors, and walls. For this reason, the down feathers from the geese and ducks that were slaughtered in late fall, and especially for Christmas dinner, filled the bedcovers and pillows. Is it any wonder that under these primitive living conditions, disease and illness were prevalent and caused great health problems and early death? But since peasants were often looked upon as nothing but a necessary evil, who were only valuable for as long as they could work for next to nothing, living conditions were not improved for them. Besides, there were always too many of them around.

Now that you understand the conditions in which my family lived, I will return to the story I alluded to. My great-grandparents, Herrman and Karoline, needed more firewood. Winters in Pomerania were rather long and cold. Their allotted firewood had almost been used up, and they had no money to buy more. Since it was common knowledge that the estate owner was a harsh and pitiless man, they did not dare ask for more. Instead, they decided to take matters into their own hands. Of course, they should have known better, since it is always questionable to take this kind of matter into your own hands. But let's face it; desperate people do desperate things. One evening, as the shadows of night were falling, they took a sharp axe and went into the woods that belonged to the estate to cut down a dead tree. Having done this, Great-grandfather heaved the heavy trunk on his shoulder while Great-grandmother took the top end of the tree and, bent under their heavy load, trudged slowly toward their abode. By now it was dark, and they were quite confident that nobody would see them. But rather soon the load on Great-grandfather's shoulder became so heavy that he had to throw it down and rest a moment. However, when they tried to lift the tree trunk up again, it seemed heavier than before, and not even their combined effort could make it budge. Now, my great-grandfather was a man used to hard and heavy labor, and he was determined to get the firewood home. Once more they tried. Their calloused hands grabbed the tree trunk anew, but try as they may, the log did not move! Just then an owl hooted nearby. Its eerie, haunting call sent cold shivers down their spines. Highly superstitious, they knew this meant bad luck, so they left the trunk, took the top end of the tree, and, as fast as their wooden clogs allowed them to run, hurried home. They were so afraid that as they rushed through the dark forest they could almost feel the devil at their heels.

The next morning all the peasants gathered on the estate yard to await their daily work assignments. Everybody was given a job except my great-grandparents. They wondered what that could mean. However, they did not have to wonder long. As soon as all the other peasants had left for their work, they were called in before the estate owner, who told them, red-faced and screaming, that they should go now and get the tree trunk home that they had left last night in the woods. Then, still shouting at the top of his voice, he warned them never to do that again. Next time he would have them mercilessly whipped before all the other peasants and incarcerated. They apologized and bowed low, as was the custom in those days, humbly promising not to do that again. Humiliated, they left and headed for the forest.

On the way to the forest, they wondered how the estate owner had found out about the theft, for they were sure nobody had seen them. And further, how would they be able to lift the heavy log today when they had been unable to do so the night before? But lo and behold, they had no problem whatsoever with lifting it onto Great-grandfather's shoulder. It appeared to them, and the circumstances seemed to attest to it, that something was not quite right with this situation. They were convinced beyond doubt that the dark woods at night were spooky. Soon the story became known to all the peasants of the estate, and all agreed that *"De Olle was mit de düvel im bund,"* which meant, "the Oldone (as the estate owner was called amongst them) was in league with the devil." And who knows, maybe he was.

*My grandparents,
Karl Heinrich and Karoline Stüwe*

Sometime around 1893 or 1894 my grandparents, Karl Heinrich and Karoline Albertine, moved from Alt-Reblin to the town of Stolp. Nobody really knows the reason for their move, but they set out to make a life for themselves away from the estate. And after a number of different jobs, Grandfather found permanent employment with the local railroad, and their life became a little easier. Grandfather and Grandmother Stüwe had two sons, Paul and Franz, and a daughter, Anna. The older of the sons, Paul, was my dad.

By the time my father was eighteen years old, the First World War raged, and he decided to answer the emperor's call and voluntarily join the Emperor's Guard. But when he showed up at the recruitment office and was examined, the sergeant in charge told him that he was not tall enough (he was two centimeters below the minimum height requirement for the Emperor's Guard) and sent him home. That hurt his pride, but it didn't get him out of military service. In 1915 he was drafted into the Emperor's Guard and saw military action in Russia, Turkey, and even Palestine, although he never made it to

Jerusalem. Toward the end of the war, when everything seemed lost, he defected from his unit and proceeded to return home. However, the military police caught him and told him that deserters would be shot at dawn unless they chose to go back to frontline duty. Naturally, he opted to return to frontline duty!

After some time of service where the fighting was heaviest, he left again for home, and this time he made it without being caught. Shortly thereafter he heard that the war was over and Germany was defeated. As a permanent reminder of that war, Dad suffered from a myriad of illnesses that would flare up from time to time. He contracted swamp fever while fighting in Turkey, and he battled cardiac asthma as well as bronchial attacks after freezing his bronchi in Russia. On account of these illnesses, he was declared a war invalid. The Romans used to say: *"Et bonum in malo!"* (there is some good in every bad thing!) The good thing about being a war invalid was that when the Second World War started Dad was not called to active duty.

Quite soon after he returned from the war, Dad married his boyhood sweetheart, Eliesabeth Glöde, and in time they were blessed with three daughters, Lotte, Lieschen, and Irmgard. Later a son, Egon, was born, but he only lived a few short hours. When the midwife saw that the baby was very weak, she told Dad to send for the minister that his son could yet receive a private baptism and would not die

My father, Paul, with daughters Lotte, Lieschen, and Irmgard (left to right)

a heathen. However, the minister tarried, and the midwife, who tried to do her utmost to keep little Egon alive, resorted to an age-old superstitious method to keep him alive. She demanded that someone fetch Eliesabeth's wedding veil, for wedding veils were believed to be powerful good luck charms. She then passed Egon under the veil several times, but to no avail. He died in her arms. When the minister finally arrived, he found himself in quite the predicament. Since the child was dead, he couldn't administer the right of baptism, which in turn meant that Egon was not a Christian, but a heathen, and no respectable minister of the church could or would, for that matter, bury a heathen!

To put it mildly, Dad was outraged when the minister told him that. After the minister left, Dad went to the gravedigger and told him his dilemma. The man had compassion and sympathy on the bereft family and provided Dad with a small coffin, and together they buried the baby. As a direct result of this experience with the Protestant clergy in Stolp, Dad broke all affiliation with that church.

While the three girls were still quite young, in 1926 their mother died of tuberculosis, which was a dreaded disease in those times. Needless to say, it was a great loss to the young family. For some time my sisters were put into an orphanage where life was very hard and impersonal. To give his daughters a home once again, Dad married in 1929; however, the wedlock only lasted for about two years before it was dissolved. This time Grandmother Stüwe looked after the girls, so they were spared a new sojourn in the dreaded orphanage. After two years, and upon the persistent urgings of his mother and sister-in-law, Emma, Dad was introduced to a young lady named Martha Völzke, an acquaintance of Aunt Emma.

When my sisters found out that Dad was going to get married again, they wept and begged him not to do so, for they feared having another stepmother like the last one. In November 1934 my father and mother were married. My sisters soon learned that their new mother loved them very much, and they lost their fear of having a new stepmother in no time.

In December 1935 I was born, and in March 1939 another sister, Renate, was added to the Stüwe family. My older sisters told me, that when I was born, my dad was intoxicated for a whole week to express his great joy and gladness that finally a son was born, the only heir, by the way, in all our kinship, to carry on the family name. And so, when friends have asked me why I don't drink any alcoholic beverages, I tell them, tongue in cheek of course, that my dad did all the drinking for me when I was born.

My earliest memories go back to the day when my sister Renate was born. I was only three years old. She, like all the rest of us, was born at home, and when the time came for my mother to deliver her, I was taken to our neighbor's home next door. After some time, I was finally ushered into our living room to see my brand new baby sister. Upon entering the room, I heard the baby cry, and I rushed over to my mother's bed to see her. I then asked where she had come from. The midwife told me that Adebar the Stork had delivered her. And to make me believe in the stork, she showed me where the nasty bird had bit my mother when he brought my little sister. Mother's leg was neatly wrapped and bandaged with a large white cloth, and as I imagined how that bite must have hurt her, I was overcome by my emotions and started to cry bitterly. Whereupon I was promptly assured by the kind midwife, that the stork's bite wasn't all that bad and my mother would soon recover. Still sobbing, I looked around and noticed that all the adults in the room had broad smirks on their faces, so I believed the kind midwife!

Chapter 2

After Dad married Mom, my grandmother moved back to live with her son Franz and his family at the edge of town. Grandmother had always been interested in spiritual things, and as a result of a series of evangelistic meetings, she was baptized in 1932 and became a member of the Seventh-day Adventist Sect, as they were called in the old country in Stolp. The baptism took place at the end of October in the Stolpe River.

Uncle Franz and Father, as well as other well-meaning folks, were afraid that Grandmother would catch pneumonia since it was late fall and the water in the river was cold. They warned her not to proceed with the baptism, but she was firm in her decision. With all her heart, she believed that her heavenly Father would take care of her as He had promised in the Bible, so she was baptized and never even got so much as a cold.

I remember my grandmother as a very loving person, like all grannies the world over. God was kind to her and allowed her to pass away some time before we had to evacuate our town, thus sparing her the unspeakable hardship and tribulation we faced while trying to escape the horrors of war.

My grandmother slept with my cousins Maria and Inge in the same bedroom. To get fresh air, they kept the window open at night. Close to the house was a streetlight that operated on gas made of coal and was highly toxic. One particular night the gas did not ignite the streetlight properly, even though the gas continued to flow. It so happened that a gentle breeze blew the gas toward the house, and some of the fumes wafted into the bedroom where my grandmother and cousins were sleeping. During the night Maria awoke and felt sick to the stomach. She called for her mother. When Aunt Emma entered the room, she immediately smelled the gas and called for Uncle Franz to come and help her get Inge and Grandmother out of the room. It took some time before Inge regained consciousness, but Grandmother had to be taken to the hospital, where she died two days later. After the incident Inge had some problems and had to be admitted to the hospital, but being young, her body fought the gas poisoning better than Grandmother, and she survived.

Grandmother's passing was a great loss for all of us but, as Pastor Brinkmann expressed it, our heavenly Father makes no mistakes. This is often hard for grieving human minds and hearts to understand, but he encouraged us that God has a master plan and is in control of the universe.

While Grandmother was living with Dad and my three oldest sisters, she urged him to go to church with them. She also tried her best to interest Dad in Bible studies with Pastor Brinkmann. After Dad married Mom, she in turn urged him not to get mixed up with that "sect." She belonged to the Evangelic Lutheran Separated Church, which was much stricter in following their beliefs than the state Protestant church. Mother did not want to have anything to do with the Sabbath keepers, for she felt that their beliefs were purely heresy. And so Dad oscillated like the pendulum of a grandfather clock for some time between the two opinions. While Grandmother tried hard to pull him to her side, my mom tried equally hard to prevent that. However, Mom let my sisters accompany their grandmother to church on Sabbaths. From time to time Pastor Brinkmann, a kindhearted and patient man, visited our family. And while Mom always found something to be busy with, he talked to Dad about Bible truths until one day Dad asked to study the Bible with him.

After studying the Scriptures for some time, Dad, under the gentle wooing of the Holy Spirit, decided, against the wishes of my mother, to follow his convictions and be baptized. The baptism took place in 1937. The congregation in Stolp had more than 100 members and was located in the Bahnhofstrasse, the Railway Station Street. Like many of the meeting places in the old country at that time, it was located in a hall and accessible only from the backyard. Although the meeting house was not grand, precious truths were preached from its pulpit each Sabbath.

My first exposure to the Seventh-day Adventist congregation in Stolp was rather brief, but it is etched forever in my memory. I remember a certain vespers in the summer of 1944 that we attended one Friday evening. If my memory serves me right, even my dear mother accompanied us. For me, this was the first religious service I can remember attending, and it made a lasting impression on my young mind and heart. However, what I remember most vividly was the fact that all the people were so kind and friendly. Why, they even noticed me, a shy little lad! Many years later when, by the prompting of the Holy Spirit, I was led to make a decision to follow Christ I remembered that vespers experience. I still thank God for those loving hearts and hands that reached out to me that Friday vespers.

Just as in the days of Jesus and the friendly fishermen from the Sea of Galilee with whom He associated,, fish was a staple food. Dad was a talented angler and could come home with a catch even when everybody else came home skunked. So fish was a rather common table fare in our home. One early morning Mrs. Krebs, the fishmonger widow, came by our street as was her custom to sell fresh flounder in the neighborhood. You could hear her from far away when she hollered her age-old advertising slogan: *"Frische fisch, frische flundern! Lüd köp frische Flundern!"* (Fresh fish, fresh flounders! Folks, come and buy fresh flounders!)

Mother bought some fresh flounders that day, which she planned to prepare for supper when Dad came home from work. Refrigeration as we know it today was not available then, so keeping perishable foods, like fish for instance, fresh over a long period of time was always risky business, but particularly during the summer. At supper the crispy brown fried flounders were served, and everybody remarked how good they tasted. My sister Irmgard, who was fourteen years old at the time, gave me my milk bottle after supper and put me to bed. She told me that I was rather picky when it came to food and that I spit out the bits of flounder I had been fed at supper.

About eleven o'clock that night, my sister Lieschen felt very sick to her stomach and threw up. Since she had a steady boyfriend, Dad accused her of being pregnant, which she vehemently denied. Around two o'clock in the morning, my sister Irmgard threw up, and shortly thereafter Mother vomited. Dad quickly realized that Lieschen was not pregnant and got really scared. While Lieschen seemed to be over the worst, Irmgard on the other hand was getting worse by the minute. So Dad put her in bed beside Mom and went to the neighbor's apartment for help. His vigorous knocking on their door aroused Mrs. Rennhack, who came to inquire what the banging was all about. Dad told her that our family was very ill and needed immediate medical attention. By now he also felt very sick. Only the rich could afford telephones in their homes, so she accompanied Dad to get the family doctor who came at once.

The doctor arrived and, after smelling the contents of the vomiting pail, asked what they had eaten for supper. He quickly deduced that the whole family was suffering from a severe case of fish poisoning. This was a very serious affliction back then. But what was really devastating to my parents was the doctor's prognosis for my sisters. He did not give them much hope of survival. Since Dad had not vomited yet, the doctor told him to go to the nearest *kneipe* (bar) and take several *Schnapps*, as there were no alcoholic drinks at home. The theory was that the alcohol would neutralize the fish poisoning. The doctor then gave each of them a liberal measure of caster oil and went home. While all this commotion and moaning and groaning was going on, I slept soundly.

Dad ignored the doctor's advice to go to the bar and get a drink to neutralize the poison. Fearing for the lives of his wife and daughters, He did the only thing a Christian would and should do in all of life's situations, good or bad. He relied on the source that never fails! He knelt down beside the big oak bed in which Mom and my sisters lay and prayed as he had never prayed before. Dad claimed the psalmist's prayer: "Call upon me in the day of trouble: I will deliver thee, and thou shalt glorify me" (Ps. 50:15). As he earnestly pleaded with God, his loving heavenly Father, he was overcome by a sweet peace and felt the assurance that his loved ones would not die but recover to full health. And recover they all did! Praise God! This experience made a lasting impression on Dad, and even in later years he fondly recalled how God had helped in the day of trouble, just like He had promised He would.

Many years later, when I was in trouble, I remembered this story and called upon God in the day of trouble and He delivered me. Yes, God is a prayer-answering God. If only we would trust Him more!

Chapter 3

The summer of 1941 my parents promised us a trip to visit my mother's sister and family. Uncle Paul and Aunt Anna Volkmann lived in the little village of Bauerhufen, only some ninety kilometers west of Stolp. Their home was very close to the blue waters of the Baltic Sea. As a young boy who liked to explore the great outdoors, I was thrilled to spend my summer vacation along a portion of the Pomeranian shoreline, which is more than 500 kilometers long.

When we arrived, I marveled at the beauty of the sandy beaches on which the swells of the southern Baltic Sea rolled ashore. Sand dunes of varying shapes, sizes, and heights were crowned with lofty trees that complemented the white sandy beaches. Underneath the broad-branched pines that grew behind the dunes, an interesting plant community flourished. The red heather, dry ground cranberries, blueberries, and crowberries were the more showy varieties. In due season all kinds of good-tasting mushrooms showed up amongst them. In other places the ground was covered with grey and green reindeer lichens, which were dried from the summer heat and would crunch, scratch, and tickle the soles of your bare feet.

The seaward sides of the dunes were mostly covered with a rather coarse, knee-high grass with razor-sharp edges. This seemed to be the only plant that was able to survive in the sandy environment. To prevent the fine sand from shifting and drifting and being blown away, *strandhafer*, a coarse grass, was planted to stabilize the dunes. Shifting sand dunes might be pleasant to the eyes of nature enthusiasts, but it can be very dangerous to everything in their proximity. It may take a long time, but eventually the shifting dunes will cover everything that happens to be in their drifting pathway, such as forests and buildings. For instance, the small village of Lebamünde in the county of Stolp was completely covered by shifting dunes in the sixteenth century.

In order to slow the erosion of the seashore, caused by the combined action of the prevailing west winds and sea currents, groynes were rammed into the sea bottom at certain intervals along the endangered shoreline to interrupt the crashing waves. Considering all the preventative measures that were taken to avoid the erosion of the coastline, it may sound highly improbable, but the rather large church of the shore village Hoff, which was built high on the steep banks above the seashore in 1250, fell victim to the destructive forces of the Baltic Sea. Mind you, this took centuries to accomplish, but in the end, the storms with their accompanying floodwaters washed away the high banks and one day the church walls came tumbling down under the screaming crescendo of the storm, much like the walls of Jericho of old.

Even though the train ride to Bauerhufen was quite exciting in itself, I do not remember too many details of the trip, for I was impatient to reach the beach. Every few minutes I would ask, "How long till we reach Bauerhufen?" We finally arrived at the train station in Alt-Banzin where Uncle Paul and cousins Hans and Günter greeted us with hugs. We then stowed the luggage in their buggy and traveled the four kilometers to Bauerhufen. We enjoyed the buggy ride tremendously. The birds were singing, thanking their Creator for the sunshine. A soft breeze blew gently, and the fresh air was filled with the fragrance of flowers and ripening grain.

Since Bauerhufen was a well-known summer resort, there were many other summer vacationers who had disembarked from the train and were traveling in buggies to the village. Like many villages in Pomerania, Bauerhufen was a typical street village where the houses and farmsteads were built along both sides of the narrow village street. The farmyards along the south side of the street bordered directly on their fields and pastures, while those along the north side lay close to the tree covered sand dunes.

Family gathering in the late 1950s.
(From left to right) My father, my nephew Klaus, my mother, my sister Renate, (unnamed), my niece Monika, Aunt Anna Volkmann, (unnamed), Uncle Paul Volkmann, cousin Günter Volkmann, and my sister Irmgard Volkmann.

Aunt Anna and cousin Charlotte greeted us in front of their house. Since we hadn't seen each other for quite some time, we exchanged heartfelt hugs. Uncle Paul and Aunt Anna's place lay on the north side of the village street. Here the dunes were very steep and high, shielding their home from the fierce winds that come down from the North in fall and winter. Big beech, oak, chestnut, and pine trees covered the dunes adjacent to their yard. On the left side of their yard stood a small barn of post-and-beam construction and covered with a thick thatch roof. Some chickens and geese ran loose around the yard. They had a large vegetable garden, complete with some huge old fruit trees as well. The famous little house with the heart in the door was aptly placed behind a large lilac bush, some distance away from the other buildings. The narrow footpath leading to this very important structure led the silent wanderer right by the neighbor's fence, behind which stood a plum tree that was pleasant to the eyes of the beholder, much like that famous tree in the Garden of Eden, for some of its fruit-laden branches stretched temptingly across the fence. And here, just as in Eden, it was declared: "Thou shalt not eat thereof!" But in the fading light of evening, things seemed to look strangely different. When the shadows of night began to lengthen, you somehow felt rather secure and wondered if the neighbor lady really said not to eat the fruit.

Does this situation sound familiar? Eve faced the same battle of appetite. Usually the tempter comes when you are least prepared for battle, not when you are ready to fight. He shows up whenever he knows you are weak. He knows too well that's when you are most vulnerable.

It was too much to bear, and I stretched out my hand until my fingers were about to touch and pick one of the ripe, yellow, juicy, delicious, but forbidden, plums. Suddenly and unexpectedly it happened; a shrill and icy female voice from the neighbor's side pierced the air and caused us to freeze where we were. It was clear that the neighbor lady had counted every single plum and knew by heart, even on the darkest night, the exact location of each golden plum on that tree. Yes, she guarded them jealously like a mother hen her chicks and seemed to cherish the moment when someone fell to the tempter's whisperings. Some folks are like that! After all, were the plums on the branches that grew across the fence really hers? It didn't matter now, because she had spotted us, and it was clear we needed to find something else to do.

Cousin Günter and I had always been rather close. We got along well and shortly after our arrival he wanted to show me his newest toy, a beautiful model of a fishing cutter, authentically crafted after the real fishing vessels so typical to the Baltic Sea. I sensed that he really liked the model. The little vessel was even rigged up with sails and seemed to invite us to just run down to the sea and play with it. But Aunt Anna kindly told us that it was not time to play yet. First, we had to eat. After the food had been put on the table and Uncle Paul had said grace, Günter and I ate as if that was our last meal. We were in a hurry to go and play; nevertheless, running away from the table after wolfing down the third piece of the irresistible, homemade *Pulverkuchen* coffee cake was simply not permitted. We had to maintain our table manners whether we liked it or not.

After all had dined and thanked Aunt Anna for the food, we finally were granted permission to leave. Cousin Günter grabbed his fishing cutter and a long cord, and off we ran to the beach. Here we put the little vessel into its element, raised the sails, and watched as it drifted away in the light breeze, securely tethered to my cousin's wrist. We rolled up our shorts, which were knee length, and walked into the water. Not long after, I noticed my mom and Lieschen, Lotte, and Renate, as well as Aunt Anna with cousins Charlotte and Hans, coming to join us on the beach. We all soon began splashing each other and running around in the shallow water, having a good time. This beat town life any day!

My older sisters were good swimmers and ventured quite far from the shore, much too far for my mother and Aunt Anna's liking. So they called them back. After enjoying the water for a bit, we turned our attention to building sandcastles. We decided to build a tall tower close to the water's edge and watch it crumble when the waves washed its base away.

In the summer Uncle Paul was the beach watchman for the shore of Bauerhufen. Amongst other duties, he had to see that all the canopied wicker beach chairs were always in good repair and rented out to the summer guests. Naturally, he had reserved one for us, and after he arrived at the beach, he showed us where it was. We quickly moved in. Most of the beach chairs were surrounded by a hip-high sand wall built by their renters to give some privacy to the beachgoer on the otherwise flat and open beach. Furthermore, one could find a little shade under the canopy to avoid burning one's skin on the first day on the beach.

We had lots of fun that afternoon, and all too soon it was time to go home. After a good supper, we were ready to go to bed, tired from all the healthy outdoor activity on the beach. Right after breakfast the next morning, Uncle Paul announced that he had to take some bags of rye to the Sorenbohm windmill and needed some "helpers." Günter and I volunteered and were ready to go immediately. Since the windmill was several kilometers away in a neighboring village, it promised to be an interesting ride by horse and wagon. Uncle Paul, himself a miller by trade, knew the millwright from Sorenbohm quite well. As soon as the horse was hitched to the wagon, Uncle Paul and cousin Hans loaded the heavy rye bags onto it. That done, we climbed aboard and began our trip. Those old country roads were narrow. They were just wide enough for two fully loaded hay wagons to pass. Most of these country roads had trees growing along both sides which, by the way, gave the rather open landscape it's own peculiar character.

Uncle Paul lived by the motto, live and let live, and that included dealing with his animals. For this reason, he didn't have a whip. Everybody seemed to have time in those days, except us young kids; we would have liked to go faster. As we rode, I looked at the fields with their ripening grain. The heavy ears bent the stalks almost to the ground. Now and then Uncle Paul would comment on the crops and how good they looked this year. Yes, God had really blessed the fields. Wild red poppies and blue cornflowers grew between the grain stalks, making for a beautiful splash of color among the yellow of the ripening grain. Suddenly a flock of grey partridge took off in front of the horse, which frightened it a bit. The young partridge were already quite large, and it was fun to watch them as they glided on stiff wings to get away from us. Shortly after this incident we turned off the road onto a field trail, a cut-off to the windmill. All of a sudden Uncle Paul stopped the horse and pointed over to the edge of the grain field where we could see a reddish-brown animal. It was a nice roe deer buck watching us. Perhaps he did not like what he saw, for without warning he leaped into the grain and disappeared from sight.

We continued our trip and before long the windmill came into view. This aroused my interest, and I peppered Uncle Paul with questions. He explained to me what the huge beam that stuck out from the backside of the mill was for. In order that the windmill could be used more efficiently, the big beam was used as a lever to turn the mill on its pivot into the direction from which the wind was blowing. As we pulled up beside the windmill, the door, which was approximately two meters off the ground, opened, and the millwright, all covered with flour dust, came out and greeted us. Then he came down the stairway and helped Uncle Paul unload the heavy bags, and together they carried them up to the milling room. Naturally, Günter and I climbed up after them.

While the millwright talked to Uncle Paul, telling him when to come and pick up the rye flour, we had a look around the milling room. There were the big millstones that ground the grain to flour. Above them was a large, wooden hopper that held the grain to be ground. Everything was covered with a thick layer of flour dust. The millwright was a very friendly man who readily answered all our questions. As we climbed down the stairs and onto the wagon, he stood in the door and waved goodbye. Rye bread, real dark rye bread, made from sourdough, was a mainstay of the Pomeranian people. Once the rye was ground to flour, Aunt Anna would bake fresh rye bread, which was always a delight to eat.

For the trip home, Uncle Paul chose a different route. Again we passed through fields of grain, potatoes, and turnips. The later being mainly used for feed even though they are an excellent source of food for humans as well. Everywhere I looked I saw farmers busy with their work, making hay while the sun was shining. After we returned from our trip to the windmill, I heard Aunt Anna say to my mom that tomorrow the fishermen would bring fresh fish, which would be a welcome change to our table. This made me think, and soon I asked Günter if he knew where the fishermen would come and unload their catch. When he told me it was in Gross Möllen, a village some kilometers east of Bauerhufen, I inquired if he would come with me and watch the fishermen work. Even though he had seen it before, he agreed to come along.

The next morning after we had eaten our *Klimpern Suppe* (lumps soup) we left for Gross Möllen. Klimpern is a dish made of rye flour that will put strength in your muscles and supposedly hair on your chest, that is, if you believed the farmhands, old-wives tales. To make the "lumps" for the soup, one first made a dough from the rye flour. The dough was then cut, and the little lumps were dropped into boiling milk. After some minutes of boiling, it was ready to be served!

When we arrived at the village, the fishermen had already pulled their small boats ashore. Together with their wives and older children, they were busy taking the flounders and butts out of the nets. There were small ones, about the size of my hand, and large ones, almost the length of my arm. The fish were sorted according to size into different crates. I looked at the fish with its eyes popping up on the same side of the head and marveled at its strange appearance. Then I remembered that just the other day I had "involuntarily" met a flounder when I was walking in the sea. We were up to our chests in the water when suddenly from underneath my foot a flounder, that was buried in the sand as their habit is in the daytime, shot forth when I stepped on it and gave me a good scare.

One of the fishermen had a horse and wagon parked alongside his boat, and as soon as the nets had been emptied and the fish sorted, he placed the crates on the wagon and went back to the village. The dunes were quite low here, but the horse still had a hard time pulling the wagon with its load up through the soft, sandy incline. Together with his wife, the fisherman drove to the different villages to sell his catch. Now I knew why Aunt Anna didn't have to come here to the beach to buy the fish she had been talking about. The fish would be delivered to her door in Bauerhufen. The other fisher families were still taking flounders out of the nets. Once this job was done, they carried the fish in baskets up the dunes to where they lived. Here they eviscerated them, tied together two flounders by their tails, and hung them over the top rails of a framework that was built for drying the fish. After hanging in the sun and rain and wind for some months, the fish were ready to be stored for later use. One has to bear in mind that to preserve food these people had only three methods: dry it, smoke it, or salt it. And that's exactly what the fishermen did with their catch that was not immediately sold or consumed.

Not far from one of the houses was a larger shack from which lots of smoke belched out. When I asked Günter if the shack was on fire, he only smiled and told me that this was their smokehouse. Here the flounders, after having been cured in a brine solution for some time, were "miraculously transformed" into those delicious *Räucherflundern* (smoked flounders), for which Pomerania was well known. While he explained this fact to me, he kept licking his lips to show me how good they tasted. Needless to say, the flounders we had for supper that day, prepared so expertly by Aunt Anna, were delicious, even though they weren't smoked

Overnight the weather changed drastically. When we got up in the morning a nasty wind was howling around the buildings, which soon grew into a full-fledged storm. Aunt Anna tried frantically to keep the doors and windows closed, but much to her dismay, the fine sand from the dunes blew in anyway. Living so close to the dunes as they did had its disadvantages in stormy weather. Uncle Paul, who had been out since early morning to look after the beach chairs, came home around noon with bad news. Almost all of the beach chairs had been buried in the wet sand and others had floated out to sea. He had tried to save as many as he could but had to retreat when the breakers came ever higher onto the beach. All day long the storm blew out of the northwest.

We kids climbed up to the crest of the dunes to see for ourselves the devastation caused by the angry sea. Some old trees on the dunes were uprooted as well. Down on the beach we could see the partly buried beach chairs. Some of them were badly broken and beyond repair. We met Uncle Paul and some other men from the village who tried anew to rescue whatever could be rescued from the beach. Wet up to their waists, they finally gave up the fight and warned us not go onto the beach because of the dangers that existed there. The sea had to calm down first. Then they would go and assess the damage that had been done.

The following morning the storm had calmed, and the Baltic Sea was smooth again. If it wouldn't have been for all the buried beach chairs and a lot of driftwood high up on the beach, you would have never known that a storm raged the day before. Beachcombers were already searching along the shore for amber, the gold of the Baltic Sea. Since prehistoric times it had been sought after by ancient cultures as far away as the Mediterranean. We boys started to look for amber too, but we didn't find any. My older sisters and cousins Hans and Charlotte were instead looking for our beach chair, which, by the way, could not be found anywhere. Some village boys, who had come to the beach, told us that a large porpoise had washed ashore on the beach of Gross Möllen.

At once, we all took off for the other village. This was something we had to see. Even my older sisters, as well as Günter's older siblings, came along. With all the company, the six kilometer walk to Gross Möllen flew by, and we arrived in no time. When we reached the beach, we saw a large crowd gathered around the creature. The poor thing was dead and half buried in the sand. Seagulls circled overhead and screamed. We figured they were only waiting for the crowd to disappear so they could inspect the carcass and fill their gizzards. While the girls put handkerchiefs over their noses and looked on from a distance, we boys had to have a closer look, regardless of the smell. I had never seen such a large sea creature before, which made it twice as interesting. We wondered if this large animal could have swallowed a man like Jonah. When the stench became too strong, we retreated to where the girls were standing. We then slowly made our way along the beach back to Bauerhufen, where we spent many more fun-filled days playing in the sand and water with our cousins.

Before we realized it, our summer vacation was over, and it was time to return to Stolp. When we arrived at the train station in Stolp, Dad and Irmgard welcomed us. When we arrived at our home, we were greeted by a pleasant surprise. Garlands hung from the ceiling in the living room, and mom's nice coffee service set was on the large oak table with a big *Pulverkuchen*. Yes, Dad was not only a talented fisherman, but he knew how to bake a delicious cake as well! It was a wonderful homecoming.

Chapter 4

Even though I was born in town, at an early age I fell in love with the countryside. I could spend hours in the meadows and woodlands with the gentle river Stolpe running through them. The animals and birds of the field and forest filled my days with joy and my young mind with never-ending questions. Of particular interest to me were the fish in the ponds and brooks. My fondest childhood recollections are of exploring the outdoors around town. The only thing that interested me in town was the museum, which was located in the *Neue Tor* (New Gate), a remnant of medieval times. Here I went mainly to look at the old stone implements like axe heads, spear points, and arrowheads as well as the clay pots and dishes from prehistoric days.

Yes, God's handiwork enriched my life at a rather tender age, and I am ever so thankful to my heavenly Father for the interest He instilled in me to appreciate His wonderful creation.

The town of Stolp had on its periphery two large forests, which were my favorite hiking locations. Even though I was quite young at the time, my parents generally never objected to my urge and interest to explore the fields and woods, as long as they knew where I was going. I am eternally thankful to them for trusting me and letting me have such freedom to express my wanderlust. Some of my friends' parents were afraid to let them roam the outdoors for fear they would get lost. My parents had no such misgivings. They knew from experience that I would find my way home. Most of the time I hiked all by myself for the very simple reason that I could do and go wherever I wanted. The *Waldkater* forest (Tomcat woods) was of particular interest to me. Within the forest a creek had been dammed in several locations, and the ponds thus created had been stocked with fish. The largest of the ponds had mirror carp and large goldfish.

However, I preferred watching the lively brown trout that lived in this creek. Here and there the current had cut deep into the sandy soil of the valley, creating steep banks as well as different sized pools. I would spend hours observing these shy fish that, at the slightest tremor on the creek bank or disturbance in the water, would dash for cover. But they would nibble at every dark object that floated by and looked remotely like food. Any insect that ventured too close to the surface of the water was a target for the agile trout, who never seemed to miss.

One day when I was sitting near the pond I observed a large trout moving ever so slowly toward the shallow part of the pool, which traditionally was the feeding place of the smaller trout. Suddenly, with lightning speed, it caught a small fingerling and swam off with his dinner. To say the least, my youthful soul was shocked and dismayed by this repulsive cannibalistic behavior of my favorite fish. From that moment on, I felt that something was wrong in the brown trout's paradise. Many years later, when I had carefully pieced together the behavior of men and beast, I came to the conclusion that both suffered from the very same cause—sin! It was sin that polluted paradise for all of God's beautiful creatures so long ago and all suffer the consequences today more than ever before. The happy hours spent beside that little brook taught me much about God's providence and care toward all of His creatures.

I was occasionally late for supper because I had completely lost track of time while watching those tantalizing trout, but that didn't bother me a bit, since I knew my dear mother would always forgive me after I apologized, although I was disciplined and corrected for my behavior. Hours later a certain part of my anatomy reminded me of my poor choice!

In my youthful innocence and perhaps simplicity, I thought that life would go on like this, that I could immerse myself in nature and learn her secrets. But the opposite was the case. Hardship and sorrow became a part of our daily lives and, to a degree, remain a part of every person's life for as long as we sojourn in this world of sin.

Since fish played a rather prominent part in my young life, I wanted an aquarium. But aquariums were impossible to get during the war unless you had "connections." Well, my parents did not have any influential friends; we were but common folk. Therefore, I got myself a large glass jar that I thought would do the job and went down to the river to do some "fishing." I knew just the right spot too. It was close to where the kayak and foldboat club had their clubhouse. This was an interesting building. With its thick thatch roof, which almost reached the ground, and its hand-carved wooden horseheads crossing on the gable ends of the roof, it had the semblance of a structure from bygone days. My fishing spot had rather shallow water and some narrow bands of reeds, which the sticklebacks seemed to like. In short, it was the right place for my venture. My "net" was a white handkerchief. I discovered that the trick was to get it underneath the sticklebacks and then pull it quickly out of the water. After trying different techniques, I became quite efficient and soon had a number of those little fish in my jar.

Upon placing them in their new home, I lay on the grass beside the jar and observed the sticklebacks. After some time I got up and started for home with my "aquarium" securely held in both hands. But, alas, before I even reached home, one of the little fish had turned belly up and was floating on the surface of the water. To say the least, I was very sad. Soon after I arrived home, another little fish had died. I was perplexed. But I did not know about the need for oxygen and clean, clear water. After Dad came home from work, I told him about my fish. He consoled me as best he could. Then he explained why the sticklebacks could not live in the jar. The water in the jar warmed up too fast and that in turn depleted the oxygen, which caused the fish to suffocate. What a revelation!

This experience did not discourage or deter me from going fishing for sticklebacks. However, now I kept the fish in the jar only long enough to observe them before releasing them back into the river. One day when I came home from such a fishing trip, I heard loud laughter coming from the backyard. I soon discovered that some of the older boys in the neighborhood had built a rather crude kayak. They were just putting on the finishing touch when I came upon the scene. Since they had been unable to obtain real canvas, after all it was wartime and real canvas was needed for more important things, they had used burlap for the outer skin of the kayak. The weave was a bit coarse, but their enthusiasm knew no bounds. It seemed that they figured the waterproofing material they were painting on would make up for the added holes of the burlap.

Even before the waterproofing substance had a chance to dry thoroughly, they took the kayak down to the river. The most daring of the bunch, amongst them our neighbor's son Horst, got into it and pushed off. But to everyone's surprise, and before they could even start to paddle, the kayak began to fill with water. The kayak's skin was clearly not watertight! Slowly but surely it dove fast like one of those dreaded U-Boats of the German Navy. Under much hooting and hollering, the "submariners" struggled to free themselves before the kayak sank completely. Like wet rats they crawled back unto the riverbank. Regardless of this mishap, we all had a swell time and a good laugh about the failed "submarine" launch.

One day in August of 1944, the last summer we spent at home, Dad told me that on Sunday he would take me fishing. Needless to say, I couldn't sleep on Saturday night. When I finally did fall asleep, I had some exciting dreams in which I caught lots of fish. Before I knew it my father was waking me up. After a short breakfast, we hopped on the train for Stolpmünde, which was eighteen kilometers north. It was in this town that the Stolpe River ran into the Baltic Sea. I knew the place well because we often spent our summer vacation there. The thirty-minute train ride, which skirted along the Stolpe River valley, went by in no time.

Upon arriving in Stolpmünde, we disembarked and walked to the harbor. We then took a ferry to the other side of the harbor. Dad knew exactly the place to fish. Moored on the quay were some old steamships that were being scrapped. We climbed on one of the old ships and got our angling rods ready. By the way, these were plain bamboo sticks, mine even without a simple fishing reel! But that did not bother me a bit. The most important thing was that we were fishing. I was a happy boy!

After Dad showed me how to put the worm on the hook so it would stay on, I set the float for the right depth, and then the angling began. Dad told me to keep the float in my sight at all times and pull when it started to bob. Well, the first time it went under, I wasn't paying attention and the fish got away. Tears filled my eyes. I checked the hook to see if the worm was still there, and it was. But the fish was gone. Dad saw what happened and told me to be more vigilant next time. A few minutes later when I saw the float go under again, I was ready. I pulled the line out of the water, and there was a beautiful fish.

But I wasn't sure how to get the fish up on the deck. The fish struggled for all he was worth; he wanted to remain in his wet domain.

I called for help, but Dad calmly told me that I had caught the fish, and I needed to land the fish. I remained determined and finally got it on the deck. It was a little over a foot long, and I felt as proud as a Spaniard. As soon as I landed the fish, Dad came over to see it. He told me it was a bream with lots of bones. Then he tapped me on my shoulder and smiled, and with that gesture I knew I had become a real "fisherman." After a while I caught another bream, and in my youthful imagination, I thought life would continue like that forever—in my simplicity I had forgotten that there was a war raging and things could change overnight.

Fishing was definitely my favorite pastime, but I also had fun picking blueberries and mushrooms, which were abundant in the month of August. One day after some good thundershowers had drenched the land and the sunshine and warmth had returned, my mom told me it was the right weather for mushrooms. In particular, the good tasting chanterelle mushrooms. She stated that the next day we would join some neighbor women and go mushroom picking. We would take the "Fiery Elijah," as the small steam train was jokingly called, and head to the little village of Labuhner Brück where mother knew of some good mushroom spots. I couldn't wait!

The next morning I pulled on my oldest clothes in preparation for crawling through the thick pine and spruce nurseries, much to the dismay of the local forester, I might add. There, in the soft green moss and reindeer lichens, grew the best chanterelles. Of course, this was also the favorite hangout of the blood-thirsty mosquitoes! But as you very well may know, one cannot have their cake and eat it too. If you wanted the mushrooms, you had to forget about the mosquitoes. It was that simple! By early afternoon our baskets were full of orangey-yellow chanterelles and we headed back to the train station. Once on board I was lulled to sleep by the jostling of the train, and in my dream I saw again the roe deer doe nurse her spotted fawns. I also saw some rather big chanterelles, and as I was about to pick them, I heard my mother call for me and I awoke. We were back in town again. That evening Mother sautéed the freshly picked chanterelles with lots of onions, and we had a feast fit for a king.

Blueberry picking was a separate adventure near the village of Reddentin, which was a few kilometers west of Stolp. Since the berries were in a state forest, one needed a permit to pick. Unfortunately, the permit cost 2,50 Reichsmark, which was a large sum of money for poor people. Nevertheless, we still made the trek to pick blueberries. Since it was a three-hour walk to the Reddentin forest, we rose at three o'clock in the morning so that we could start picking berries by six. This was necessary to avoid the tormenting horseflies, deerflies, mosquitoes, and sandflies. By eleven o'clock one had to leave the forest if one wanted to avoid becoming a "pincushion" for the airborne tormentors. Since there were also common vipers in the woods that could deliver venomous bites, you had to wear ankle-high boots and knee-high socks into which you tucked your pant legs.

You might wonder if it was worthwhile to pick berries under such circumstances. However, the other side of the coin is that many poor people were able to earn some much-needed cash by picking and selling good mushrooms and berries. Of course, we also enjoyed the extra special food. My mom cooked most of the blueberries that we picked and preserved them in bottles and jars. Some berries would be mixed with milk and sugar and eaten for dessert.

Chapter 5

My older sisters, Lotte and Lieschen, both got married during the last years of the war. When my brothers-in-law were sent to the front lines to fight in the senseless war, Lotte moved in with her in-laws, while Lieschen stayed with us at home.

Lotte's wedding took place in the little town of Gross Garde by the lake of Garde. Most people in the town made a living by farming and to a lesser degree by fishing. In fact, the lake was well known for its peculiar shaped fishing boats. Since the acreage of the common farm was usually very small, the farmers had to look for another source of income and the lake, with its abundance of fish, lent itself to this purpose.

After the church service, we all went to my sister's in-laws' farm where the wedding reception was held. Even though the war was already raging and food might have been scarce in the larger cities, the wedding dinner showed no sign of any such shortage. After dinner I went outside to have a look around. I was more interested in the lakeshore and the reed beds with their teeming birdlife than to listen to what the adults were talking about. I befriended another young lad who had come with his parents to the wedding and together we made our way along the cobblestone street down to the lakeshore were the fishing boats were moored. It smelled like tar and seaweed and rotten fish. Some fishing nets hung on poles to dry. As we got closer to the nets, we suddenly realized where the rotten fish smell was coming from. The fishermen must have forgotten to wash their nets before hanging them up to dry.

We watched the seagulls glide effortlessly in the wind and enjoyed the noise of the many birds that were nesting in the reed beds. Some coots and ducks swam close to the reeds as a large osprey flew over them looking for fish. What a magnificent bird! We then climbed aboard one of the boats that had been pulled ashore and imagined we were sailing to where our nets were in the water, full with fish. Years later when I read about the Sea of Galilee, of Simon Peter and the other hardy fishermen, my mind immediately jumped to my childhood memories of the peaceful shores of Lake Garde with its fishing boats and fishermen. We were awakened from our daydreaming by my dad's voice calling me to say goodbye to my sister Lotte, for it was time to board the train and return to Stolp.

The next time I saw Lotte and her family was almost ten years later in 1955 when the whole family came to visit us in what had become West Germany. You see, my sister, her son, and her in-laws, as well as millions of other people from Pomerania and East Prussia, were expelled from their homes after the war as Joseph Stalin reorganized Eastern Europe as he saw fit.

In the summer of 1944 wagon trains came rolling through our town. It reminded everyone that the awful, dreaded storm clouds of war were getting closer all the time. The people fleeing from the frontline of fighting in East and West Prussia talked a strange dialect that sounded funny to us kids. When I asked my parents about them, I was told that they were refugees who had lost their homes because of the war. Everywhere we went, we heard about the war and saw a piece of its horrible effects. Lucky for us, East Pomerania had no important industries and had escaped the devastating bombings that other parts of Germany had suffered. What we did not escape, however, was the propaganda of the Third Reich. "Give more for the war effort!" We were encouraged to collect anything and everything like old paper, scrap iron, rags, and even bones to help win the war.

More often than before, my parents sat beside our new radio, which they had obtained through some connections of my sister Lieschen, in the evenings listening to the latest news. They would tightly press one ear against the loudspeaker because the volume was turned so low that you hardly heard a thing. I wondered about their strange behavior. This was in the time when virtually everything was prohibited. Naturally, it was strictly prohibited, in fact, by threat of death, to listen to any allied radio station that broadcasted in German. Persons caught doing so were mercilessly imprisoned.

It became difficult to know whom you could trust. Some sly and sordid townspeople would run around after dark and spy on their neighbors. They did not shy away from putting their ears to people's windows in order to find out what the inhabitants were saying. If they heard anything about politics or the war that was or could be construed as anti-Nazi government, they turned their neighbors over to the authorities, which resulted in coupons for groceries and the like. The Gestapo would then arrest the people in question, interrogate them, and send them to concentration camps, which many never returned from.

My dad did not belong to the Nazi Party, and one day he shared some of his convictions with his co-workers. He crossed the boundary of keeping all political matters to yourself, and he almost paid dearly for his moment of venting. A coworker betrayed him and Dad was arrested. The Gestapo determined that he should be sent to a concentration camp. However, God compelled some of Dad's friends to intervene on his behalf, and the Gestapo dropped the charges against him. We praised God for His kindness and mercy in saving Dad from the death camps.

This incident was not the only time Dad narrowly escaped being sent to a concentration camp. One day Dad was leaving a store in downtown Stolp when a column of Brownshirts, complete with band and banners, marched by. This was the signal that all people on the sidewalk and street were to salute and shout *"Heil Hitler!"* (Hail Hitler!) It was compulsory! However, Dad felt that in this way he was giving Hitler allegiance as to a god. He thought of the three Hebrew youth who determined not to bow to Nebuchadnezzar's idol even if God wouldn't protect them from the wrath of the king and vowed not to honor Hitler. In order to not draw attention to himself, Dad snuck quietly along the narrow walkway between the houses that led to the back alley. But one of the Brownshirts saw him and together with some other men started running after Dad. They shouted at him to come back and salute the flags. Dad did not answer them but kept on running. This made them even more angry. After a few minutes they gave up the chase, but they threatened him that they knew who he was and would come pick him up later and take him to the concentration camp. The next few days were very apprehensive as we waited to see if the men really knew who my father was and would indeed arrest him. Fortunately, they never showed up at our home.

If my parents would have been caught listening to the American Forces broadcast, one can only guess what would have happened to them. Thank God no one ever found out or reported them! They took the risk in order to obtain accurate news about the war. German radio stations only fed listeners the official propaganda, which was nothing but a bunch of lies. If one believed the reports, the war was as good as won. In order to be informed on how the war was really going, you had to listen to the allied broadcast. When one lives in a totalitarian state where almost everything is prohibited, including loving your neighbor as yourself, it is not exactly easy to be a practicing Christian and not be in conflict with the authorities. You have to choose between the "thus says the Lord" and the dictates of the state.

One morning a heavily guarded column of POWs was in our immediate neighborhood to do some work. Because it was summer and we were out of school,

My sister Lotte Grunst with her husband Karl and their children Eckart, Willi, Hannchen and Annemarie – summer 1955.

a bunch of us kids soon gathered around to watch. We tried to identify the country of origin of the POWs by their badly worn uniforms and by listening to them speak. The French seemed to be the most jolly of the bunch. Some were even singing. Almost all were quite friendly to us kids. On the other hand, the Russian prisoners seemed to be the most pitiful. Their inexpressive faces told of the hardship they had gone through. One Russian word stuck in my young mind, perhaps because we heard it so many times. *"Hlyeb!"* (Bread!) Their hollow eyes begged for food, and our young hearts yearned to help. But we knew better. No one dared to help, for this was strictly prohibited and we feared getting caught.

Around noon the guards marched the POWs back to camp, but they left an old Russian and one guard behind. At that moment my mother came looking for my sister Renate and me and told us to come home for dinner. As we were about to leave, the old man asked my mom in broken German for some bread. He said he was very hungry. If I remember correctly, all he had with him were some cold, boiled potatoes. His pleading request cut right through my mother's heart. We hurried home, and Mother readied a large bowl of hot soup from the pot she had on the table, as well as some sandwiches. Before leaving the house, she looked to see if the guard was around. It appeared that the guard had disappeared. Quickly she gave me the food that she had securely packed in a handbag and told me to run over to the old man and give it to him, all the while reminding me to be careful not to spill the soup. She kept a lookout for the guard while I took the food to the old man.

When he saw what I had brought him, he almost smothered me with his overwhelming thanks. The old man hungrily wolfed down the food while I waited for the bowl and handbag. A thankful smile brightened his wrinkled countenance when he finished, and he again thanked me in his native tongue, "*Spacieba, spacieba!*" (Thanks, thanks!) I was still standing there and listening to the old gentleman when my mother's shouts brought me back to action. I fetched the empty bowl, put it into the handbag, and ran as fast as I could back to my mother. At that moment I saw the guard appear, but he did not suspect anything. We were lucky. No one turned us in for this act of civil disobedience.

My sister Lieschen Draheim with her husband Gerhard, and son Wolfgang

Toward the end of 1944 and in early 1945, Stolp had the occasional bombardment. Because our town had no important industries or railroad yards, no one knew why the bombers hit us. The few instances happened at night. When the well-known mournful wail of the sirens went off, my parents and older sisters would jump up and quickly dress themselves. Then they would get my younger sister Renate and me out of bed and dress us too. Next, we would all rush across the street to the basement of the Jewish senior citizens' home, which was the designated bomb shelter for our area. There we would sit with other neighbors on chairs and benches, trying to get some sleep. Others would play cards or talk about the approaching bombers and how they would destroy everything. Some of the small children and babies cried. After what seemed like an eternity the sirens would wail again, telling us that the danger was over for this time. When the all-clear was signaled, everyone breathed a sigh of relief and quickly dispersed to their homes to catch up on the lost sleep. The only bomb damage was usually inflicted by some small, two-engine, Russian bombers. Luckily they had only a limited amount of "fireworks," and their aim was not all that accurate either. All in all, Stolp received very little bomb damage during the war.

The one bombing that did the most damage was when a bomb fell on some large storage sheds full of carbide. As soon as they hit their target, the sheds exploded, throwing the carbide into the air. Some fell in a nearby ditch that contained some water and acetylene gas immediately developed. The gas mixture ignited when some burning debris from the shed fell in the water. Soon the whole area was one big inferno that lit up the dark night sky. The local firefighter brigade was alerted to the fire and arrived on the scene in short order and quickly extinguished the blaze. The next day after school some of the boys from the neighborhood and I went to see the damage. Some of the ashes were still smoldering, and the air was yet heavy with the stink of acetylene gas.

One morning we noticed that the Jewish senior citizens' home was unusually quiet. Nobody was moving inside or outside the building. Soon the devastating news surfaced that the elderly occupants had been driven away in trucks in the middle of the night. I heard my parents whisper that most likely they had been taken away to the concentration camp. This dreadful thought was always uppermost on everyone's mind who was not connected with the Nazi Party. My parents, as well as some of the neighbors, were really upset and concerned about the disappearance of the senior citizens, but they were powerless to do anything about it. If they inquired or complained to the authorities, they might end up there too.

The war was much closer to home and was now impacting our community, but I had no idea how much more change was in store for our family. One day as I played with the livery barn my dad had made for me for Christmas Mother kept telling me I was in her way. She and Lieschen and Irmgard were packing clothes and bedding stuff into wooden trunks. Chinaware and other breakable glassware and dishes were packed into the bedding for protection. When I asked if we were moving, I did not receive an answer. That wasn't like my mother at all. Now I really wondered what was going on. The mysterious packing continued for a few more days, but I still didn't know what was happening. Then on the afternoon of March 6, 1945, a large truck stopped in front of the old two-storied apartment building we lived in. Some men came to the door and talked to my mom. They loaded the trunks on the truck and off they went. That evening after my dad returned from work he took me on his knee and told me that we were moving. But that was all he would say.

My dad had worked for many years as a civilian on the local Luftwaffe airfield in Reitz, about six kilometers east of Stolp. The airfield commander had received orders to vacate the airfield with all his staff. This order was the reason for the mysterious packing activity at home. That evening we kids went to bed early. However, before Mom and Dad went to bed, they listened to the radio. Some allied station broadcast information about the advancement of the Russian army with their formidable P34 tank brigades just fifteen kilometers southeast from Stolp in the village of Rathsdamnitz. My parents were very disturbed by this news, for they feared that we would not be able to get away before the Russians arrived in Stolp. During the night the wail of the sirens signaled an air raid. As was our custom, we ran across the street to the Jewish senior citizens' home for shelter.

As soon as the sirens sounded the all-clear signal, two Brownshirts came into the bomb shelter and announced to everyone's utter surprise that the Russian tanks had broken through the German defense line at Rathsdamnitz and were on their way toward Stolp. The town had to be evacuated. Everybody had to go to the local branch of the Nazi Party office or city hall and get their evacuation papers. This devastating news shocked almost everyone in the bomb shelter, except my parents. While my older sisters went to fetch the permission papers to leave Stolp, the rest of our family went back home. It sure was a sad moment for my parents. The uncertainty of the future weighed heavily on their hearts. Would we ever come back to our beloved town and home? Since my parents were only allowed to take the most necessary things along, all the furniture and most of the clothes and other belongings remained behind. The radio also stayed behind.

Dad was mad about many things. Above all, he was mad at the Nazis who had brought all this turmoil and hardship upon millions of innocent people in order to satisfy their hunger for power and revenge. As my sisters were returning from city hall, they met a young woman with two little children who was looking for the camp of the Reichs Arbeitsdienst, the conscripted Reichs Labor Service. The children were crying and the woman was close to tears as well. My sisters tried to comfort them and went with her to help her find the place. Even though they needed to come home themselves, they felt compelled to help this woman first.

After assisting the young woman, they once again headed for home. Making their way through the dark streets, they heard the deep noise of a motor that could only come from a tank. Their next thought left them shuddering with fear: Was it a Russian tank? Their first reaction was to run away, but then they looked back, and to their relief they noticed the German emblem on the tanks turret. Two German tanks that were unable to fight any longer came slowly into town. My sisters' fear turned into joy.

Lieschen and Irmgard finally arrived home at about six o'clock in the morning. They were just in time to come with us to the airfield Reitz. The officer in charge had sent cars to town to pick up the staff who lived there. However, my dad and Irmgard used their bicycles to get to Reitz. When Irmgard got to the airfield, she stood at the entrance gate and watched the seemingly never-ending stream of soldiers and refugees trudging by on the road to Lauenburg, fifty kilometers from Stolp. Suddenly an army vehicle stopped and out jumped a soldier. But she knew that it was Uncle Franz who was standing before her. He was very much astonished, perhaps even confounded, to see my sister at the gate. Irmgard ran at once to get Dad so that he could talk to his brother. The conversation was brief, since Uncle Franz had come to get his superior and, regrettably, had no time for anything else. But the brief encounter was a blessing. With a heavy heart and tears in their eyes the brothers parted after a few minutes, unsure of what the future held for any of them.

Close to noon my mom wanted to prepare something for dinner, but she found that they had forgotten the potatoes at home. Irmgard volunteered to ride back to town on her bike to fetch the potatoes. Dad didn't want Irmgard going alone, so he jumped on his bike too and went after her. When they arrived at our apartment, Irmgard went down into the cellar to get the spuds. Dad looked sadly around the living room when suddenly his eyes caught the radio. Something got into him, and he went to the shed in the backyard, got an axe, and smashed the back of the radio, breaking all the tubes into hundreds of pieces. From the front the radio still looked good. He then returned the axe to the shed.

Meanwhile, Irmgard picked enough potatoes and was about to leave the cellar when she heard someone open the living room door. To her utter surprise, Lotte walked in. At the same time Dad came back from the shed and, he too, was shocked to see Lotte. He asked her where she had come from and what she needed. She told him that she had come to take our family to Gross Garde so that we could be all together when the Russians came. She figured that we could hide in the reed beds along the lakeshore or on the islands. Dad told her it was impossible for him to do so because he had orders to retreat with the air force civilian staff and if he disobeyed the order he would be shot. Dad asked her where Eckart, her infant son, was. She told him that he was with her in-laws in Gross Garde. That made Dad and Irmgard very sad, and they all cried bitterly. Dad had hoped to take Lotte and her young son along with us to Reitz so that we all could flee together. After many hugs, tears, and kisses, they parted, uncertain if they would ever see each other again. Lotte went back to her in-laws, and Dad and Irmgard came back to Reitz.

When Mom and Lieschen heard what had happened, they too started to cry. What heartrending moments for the whole family. In late afternoon all the important installations on the airfield were destroyed and shortly thereafter the command was given to leave. However, there was only one problem, the orders read to retreat to Strahlsund in West Pomerania, but since the Russians had practically closed off that escape route, there was no way to follow this command. Together the leading officials of the airfield decided that, in order to get away, we had to move east toward the city of Danzig.

The road leading away from Reitz was thoroughly congested. Two rows of military convoys and one row of refugees, as well as many pedestrians with handcarts between the vehicles, filled the road. It took our little convoy all night to cover the forty-four kilometers from Reiz to Lauenburg. My dad, his superior, and other senior staff were in the first truck. All the women and children were in the second truck. Both trucks had makeshift canopies of plywood to keep out the wind, snow, and cold. The third truck carried all the baggage and was driven by my dad's friend, Uncle Wilhelm Adam. Lieschen and Irmgard also rode in that truck. Because we had access to transportation, we had a realistic chance of getting away from the advancing Russian army; however, many of our close neighbors and friends regrettably did not.

Many years after the war we heard from a neighbor, Horst Rennhack, in a letter addressed to my dad about their ordeal. He wrote: "We were three days into our flight when we were overtaken by the Russian army. Therefore, we returned to Stolp. The Bokelows [neighbors who lived above us] arrived one day later, but without their son Siegfried. He had been shot by Russian soldiers in the village of Jeseritz while trying to shield his sixteen-year-old sister Giesela from being raped by those barbarian soldiers. While plowing his field, a farmer found him in his shallow grave. My brother Rudi got killed in the last days of the war. In the summer of 1947 we were herded like cattle into railcars by the Poles and expelled to the D.D.R, German Democratic Republic, from which I have escaped some time ago."

Around six o'clock in the morning we finally arrived in the town of Lauenburg. The night had been rather cold and snowy. Upon arriving in town, Dad, in his capacity as convoy leader, had to go and find lodging for us. The only place that had the authority to grant such lodging was the local branch office of the Nazi Party. He found the chief of the Brownshirts at a drinking party. He was dressed in his best uniform and decorated with all his distinguished badges and surrounded by a swarm of women. Needless to say, everyone was drunk. When Dad presented his request, he was told that there was no room for any more refugees in Lauenburg. Dad got upset over this man's attitude toward the refugee situation and got into a heated argument with him. But before it got too hot, Dad's superior appeared and calmed him down. He pulled Dad out of the place and told him that it wasn't worthwhile to argue with a drunk German soldier and perhaps be shot in the end.

We took a short break to eat and drink and stretch our legs before continuing our trip. After some time we arrived in the small village of Reda. Here the inhabitants had already prepared themselves to capitulate. White bed sheets as well as other white flags hung from windows and flagpoles. During the day we were constantly under fire by the artillery and ground-support airplanes. Since the main line of defense was rather close by and the Russian army was expected to overrun the village shortly, we unanimously decided to continue our trip. The convoy drove toward Gotenhaven and from there on to Zoppot, both small towns by the Baltic Sea. We could see several large German navy vessels some distance off shore.

It seemed as if there was nowhere to hide. When we neared the town of Gotenhaven we found that a fierce tank battle was raging. Many civilians were looking for a place of safety from the battle and were streaming from the area on to the roads. Besides the heavy fighting on the ground, an equally fierce battle was fought in the air. All the time we were under fire from ground support fighter aircraft. This forced us many times to leave the trucks and look for shelter in the basements of houses that stood by the side of the road. One time when the trucks stopped and we fled for cover, our family got separated. My dad, Lieschen, and Irmgard ran one way, and my mother, Renate, and I went in the other direction because we were in different trucks and the one we were on had driven a little further then the others before the driver stopped.

After the battle noise calmed down somewhat, my older sisters came out from the relative safety of the bomb shelter they were in to search for us. My dad was in poor shape. He had mostly walked beside the trucks, often in the water-filled ditches beside the road, to clear the way for our convoy, and now his rheumatism flared up, which made it almost impossible for him to walk. As a child Dad had survived two bad cases of rheumatic fever. It was late afternoon when we got separated, and my sisters searched all night for us from house to house and in all the basements. Toward morning they finally found us. What a relief that was for Mother and them.

In the confusion of that same stop, Dad's superior lost his eighty-year-old mother, and even though many of our party helped him search for her, she could not be found. What that poor man went through emotionally in the moments and hours that followed, nobody but God knows. Simply put, he was devastated. In the early morning hours, my older sisters, together with Uncle Wilhelm Adam, went back to the trucks to get some food for us.

Since the ground support fighter planes were again strafing the town, a smoke screen was created to disable them from finding any targets. But it also made it harder for people to find their way around. Uncle Adam, who apparently did not see where he was going, fell into a hole in which a container with chemicals smoldered, creating the artificial fog. Even though my sisters pulled him out immediately, the acid had burned his knee and elbow. He had lost his cap in the fall and was determined to get it back. Against the sound advice of my concerned sisters, he crawled back into the acrid smoke of the pit to search for it. When he finally found it, the cap had largely been destroyed by the acid. Uncle Adam's wounds began to bother him, and he groaned and moaned incessantly in pain. My sisters suggested that they go to a military hospital, but he adamantly declined. When they arrived back at the bomb shelter with the food, we ate a good breakfast.

Since the fighting continued and there was no lodging for refugees, the superior gave the order to continue with the retreat. However, before we boarded the trucks, everyone did one more search of the town for his mother. To everyone's regret, we did not find her and had to leave without her. When we finally arrived in Zoppot, we were greeted with another air raid, so we ran to the nearest bomb shelter, which happened to be close to the train station in a large house. The bombardment was very fierce, and as if this was not enough, the Russian artillery started to shell Zoppot as well. After the bombing and shelling had calmed down a little, some men came into the bomb shelter and informed us that the Russians had broken through the German defense line on a breadth of about eleven kilometers and were advancing fast. Everybody had to leave Zoppot immediately. They told us to go to a certain pier to be evacuated. However, by this time my dad was so ill and could not move, so we stayed right there in the bomb shelter awaiting our fate. We knew we were in the Lord's hands, and He always knows what is best for us and is closest when all help seems to have vanished.

The next day my older sisters found a medical doctor who came to examine Dad. After checking him over, the doctor admitted him to a military hospital. Against all odds, the feared Russians did not show up—the Germans had miraculously stopped their advance. We thanked God for His protection that evening. We didn't know how fortunate we were to be alive until after we learned of the fate of the rest of our friends who had boarded the ships that left that day to take them across the Baltic Sea to safety. We learned that their ship was hit by Russian torpedoes and sank, killing the thousands of refugees and wounded soldiers on board.

With most of the townsfolk evacuated, it was rather quiet in the bomb shelter. Mom and my older sisters talked about our present situation. They decided they would not leave without Dad, no matter what happened. Mom and Lieschen decided to go to the hospital the next day and see how Dad was doing. Irmgard was assigned the duty of staying with Renate and me in the bomb shelter. When Mom and Lieschen got to the hospital, they found the place deserted. All of the nursing staff had gone. Only those patients who were unable to walk had been left behind in the basement and had been told not to worry, for they would be well taken care of. What a bunch of lies! Also, there was no electricity in the building, which made it difficult to find one's way around. Not knowing where they had taken Dad, Mom called for him until he heard her and answered.

Once they were reunited he told her that we would have to go on by ourselves since he was yet too weak to walk and he no longer had any clothing for they had taken his clothing off and placed him in a hospital gown. Mom and Lieschen searched for his clothes, which was no easy task in the dark. However, after some time of groping around in the darkness, they finally found some of Dad's clothes, as well as a ladies' shirt, and soon they had him dressed and ready to go.

Meanwhile, Irmgard rushed up from the basement of the house many times to see if they were coming. Disappointed when she did not see them, she would run down the steps again to stay with us. The night was pitch black, and she thought she heard distant rumblings that sounded like noise from a panzer. This frightened her all the more since she feared that it came from the advancing Russian tanks. In her fear of being found and captured, she cried almost the whole night. Finally around five in the morning, the door opened and Dad called for her. That was a great relief for Irmgard and us. Again the tears flowed freely; however, this time for joy.

In the two days that Dad had been in the hospital, he had, against all hope, recuperated enough that with support from Mom and Lieschen he was able to limp from the hospital to the house in which we stayed. Praise God that the German army had kept the advancing Russians at bay long enough for us to plan our next move. Psalm 34:7 had new meaning for our family: "The angel of the Lord encampeth round about them that fear him, and delivereth them."

Dad asked Irmgard and Lieschen to go to the pier and see if the vessels were still evacuating civilians. My sisters immediately left for the pier. When they reached it, a few ships remained, and the sailors told them to hurry and get on board. The Russian artillery was shooting again, and the navy vessels needed to head out to safer water. My sisters replied that they could not come right then because they needed to fetch their parents and younger siblings first. Again the sailors told them to hurry, so my sisters lost no time and ran back to the bomb shelter.

As soon as they arrived, they informed us of the situation, and we each grabbed the few belongings we had—our rolled-up sleeping blankets and a rucksack full of dried bread; everything else remained in the trunks on the trucks—and started for the pier. However, Dad was not able to walk fast, so it took some time to reach the water's edge. As we walked the artillery shells whistled over our heads. We were afraid that they might hit us. Whenever they fell into the sea, they instantly created huge fountains of water, and when they hit the ground, dirt and debris flew into the air. Now and then they fell quite close, and whenever the whistling overhead sounded too close for comfort, we would hit the ground.

We finally reached the pier and were horrified when we saw that the sailors were about to loosen the ropes with which the vessel had been moored. Would they leave without us? We tried to hurry even more, yelling to them to wait for us. In our haste we almost fell into one of the gaping holes that the artillery shells had made in the pier's planking. I was terrified by this experience and started to holler and cry at the top of my lungs when I saw the murky seawater through the huge hole. I suddenly realized that I could not swim, and in that same thought I realized what the artillery shells could do to the ship! I was scared to death!

Two of the sailors ran over to where I was fighting with my sisters to get away from the damaged pier and the ship. I was not willing to lose my life at such a young age. When they grabbed me, I fought them with tooth and nail. I clawed and kicked wildly, but the husky young fellows subdued me in short order and then carried me onto the navy vessel. When I saw that Mom and Dad and my sisters boarded right behind me, I calmed down somewhat. The sailors turned me loose below deck and told me to take it easy. They assured me we would never get hit by the Russian artillery because their aim was too poor. However good their intentions were, this assurance did not pacify me in the least.

As soon as we were on board, the naval captain gave the orders to leave. Under heavy artillery fire, we headed out to sea. From Zoppot we traveled without any disruptions to Danzig Neufahrwasser, where we arrived in the late afternoon. Here all the refugees were escorted from the navy ships into the huge harbor storage halls that were beside the docks. As soon as we got inside the hall, we looked for a place to sit or lay down. The floor was cold, dirty, and filled with other refugees trying to get some rest.

Soon after our arrival in the hall, the military police showed up looking for old men and young boys among the refugees to enlist in the "glorious" Volkssturm, Hitler's last ditch effort to "win" his war. All prospects were told to step out of the hall to be taken by truck to the nearest recruitment center. They were told that they were needed to stop the advance of the Red Army, a feat that the regular army was seemingly unable to accomplish. Although it did not seem logical that old men and boys could do something that trained men could not, the Nazi Party was clearly desperate. Dad showed the men his discharge papers from the army and told them he was sick, but they still told him to go outside.

A young couple lay beside us. The young man had been discharged from the army because of a shot to the head. To complicate matters, his wife was pregnant with their first child. After the military police officer inspected his papers, he told him in a stern voice that knew no mercy that he was good enough to fight in this last campaign. The poor women lamented and cried her heart out but that did not impress the stone-faced and heartless officer in the least. We waited the whole night for the men to return, hoping that the officers would see how totally unfit they were for army service, but we waited in vain. Nobody returned.

The next morning when I had to go to the bathroom, my sister Irmgard came along with me. After doing my business, on the way back to the hall we ran straight into the stern-faced officer who had taken Dad away. When my sister recognized him, she asked him where the men had been taken to. He told her that they had been bussed to the army barracks in Danzig-Langfuhr where they would be examined to determine if they were good enough to fight in the war. He said they were needed for the defense of Danzig.

Irmgard asked him how come he, as a healthy man in the prime of life, was not serving on the first line of defense in Danzig. Naturally, he did not answer her. That, more than anything, stirred her anger, and she told him that if he planned to win the battle with the old men, boys, and invalids he had dragged out of the halls, he was out of his mind. She told him that the Russians would be here in a few short days and then he would have to face the music himself. That seemed to strike the right cord, for he hollered at her to be quiet or else he would arrest her on the spot. But it isn't the Stüwe's manner to capitulate in the face of danger, and instead of being silent, she told him that in that case the war would at least be over for her. When he heard that, his mouth fell open in disbelief. While he thought of what to say or do next, we disappeared into the crowd of refugees that had gathered around us.

Chapter 6

After Irmgard returned me to Mother, she asked Lieschen to accompany her to the army barracks of Danzig-Langfuhr. When they arrived, they had no problem finding the barracks, for they were surrounded by trenches in which the soldiers were ready for the defense. However, they were unable to find an entrance anywhere. One of the soldiers in the trench asked why they were walking around the barracks. Irmgard told him that they were looking for the entrance. Whereupon he wanted to know what business they had there. He told them civilians were not permitted inside. When Irmgard told him that they wanted to see their father who had been taken by the military police for an examination, all the soldiers in the trench started to roar with laughter. At once an officer appeared and demanded to know what was going on. His soldiers told him that the two *Fräuleins* were looking for their dad who was in the barracks to be examined to see if he was able-bodied to fight the Red Army, and again they laughed.

The officer told them to shut up, and then, turning to my sisters, he told them where they should go to find Dad. He then saluted them and left. What a different behavior as compared with the bully from the military police. There were many barracks in the yard, but they picked the one closest to them, and believe it or not, it turned out to be the right one. To get inside the barrack, they had to pass by a guard who sat in a guardroom. He seemed to be busy with something important, so they attempted to sneak by him. But that was a mistake, for instantly he opened the sash window and shouted at them that civilians were not permitted in the barrack. But Irmgard was not in the least intimidated by his shouting; instead she asked him if this was the place where the men were examined for the Volkssturm.

Although still fuming with rage, the guard told her that this was the place she was looking for. He then informed her that the examination started at eight o'clock. Irmgard thanked him for the information and then went to sit down with Lieschen on one of the long benches that lined the hallway. Lieschen could not bear the stress any longer and started to cry. At eight o'clock the swinging doors opened and Dad appeared in the hallway. Seeing his daughters on the bench and Lieschen crying, he was overcome by his own emotions and started to cry too. Regaining his composure, he asked them what they were doing there. When Irmgard told him that they had come to get him out of there, he said there was no chance they would let him go. He told the girls to return to Mom and try to get away on our own. But he did not know his daughter—she was determined to keep the family together.

Irmgard told him that he should simply come along with them, whereupon Dad explained to her that that was out of the question. If he were to leave, he would be shot on the spot. Irmgard then assured him that she would try everything in her power to get him out of there, even if she had to tear the place apart. Dad tried to calm her down, but by now all three were crying bitterly. Dad was tired and in a lot of pain, for he could not stand on his feet for very long. My sisters tried to find a chair for him just as the registration process began. The officer in charge did not say a word at first; he only looked at them in disbelief. Finally he turned toward Irmgard and asked her what she was doing there. In her resolute way, she told him that she had come to retrieve her sick father, for he was very ill and could hardly walk. She told him that only three days ago he had still been in a military hospital. She went on to tell him that he was a war invalid from the First World War.

After patiently listening to her, the officer asked Dad for his discharge papers from the army. It took him only a few minutes to read them, then he looked at Dad and asked him why in the world he was there, for his papers plainly stated that he was unfit for active service. However, he regretted that he could not let him go. He would have to go through with the examination, and with that he put a stamp on the papers and sent him to another barrack.

My sisters accompanied him there also. While they were crossing the yard some ground-support fighters flew over the barracks. A soldier shouted to them that they should run to the bomb shelter. Irmgard told Lieschen to run for the safety of the bomb shelter, but she remained with Dad, who, because of his stiff legs, was unable to negotiate any stairs. When the soldier saw that they did not heed his advice, he got very mad at them.

After the planes left, Dad and Irmgard went into the barrack for the next examination. While Dad took off his coat and shirt, the doctor read his discharge papers. After reading them, he told Dad to get dressed again, put another stamp on the papers, and told him to go to the next station in another barrack. Germans are known for obeying rules and regulations, and this certainly was a good example of it. Why these two officers, after reading his discharge papers and seeing the state he was in, did not tell him to leave is beyond any logical understanding.

Before heading to the next barrack, Irmgard went to get Lieschen out of the bomb shelter. Since the examining doctor did not say anything to Dad, his hopes of getting out of there had vanished completely, and he told my sisters that they should head back to their mother. But Irmgard told him that they would not leave him. They entered the next barrack and soon stood before one more officer. After reading Dad's papers, he said, "Dear man, for you the war is over." With that, he wrote some discharge remarks on the papers, stamped them anew, and Dad was released and free to go.

At that moment, Irmgard felt as if a big rock fell from her shoulders as the tension vanished and Dad, suddenly released from the huge emotional burden and stress that he had been carrying, broke into tears of joy. Again and again Dad said that he could not comprehend how Irmgard had been able to get him out of the army barracks. Dad's seventy-year-old colleague from work was not that lucky; he was deemed fit to serve in the Volkssturm. He had to stay in Danzig-Langfuhr to stem the Russians that were coming closer and closer. Dad bade his old friend farewell, and in tears they parted, knowing they would never see each other again.

Since it was important to return as soon as possible to the harbor halls of Neufahrwasser where Mom with Renate and I were anxiously waiting, Irmgard and Lieschen placed Dad between them so that he could lean on them and walk a little easier. In order to get out of the army barracks, they had to exit the same way they had entered, which meant passing by the soldiers who had harassed them early that morning. When they walked by the trench in which the soldiers were, their eyes popped out since they remembered all too well that they had told the girls they were crazy to try and retrieve their father. Irmgard's victory knew no bounds. She looked down on the poor soldiers in their trench and said to them, with a jubilant voice that was full of sweet victory and pride, "I told you I would get my dad out of here; now I have him." All were quiet this time.

But getting Dad released from the Volkssturm and getting him back to us were two different things. As they soon found out, he could hardly walk. They quickly decided that Irmgard would go to the next house that still seemed to be occupied and beg for a cane for Dad. When she knocked at the door, there was no answer, so she opened the door and called to see if anybody was home. Soon an elderly woman came and asked what she wanted. Irmgard told her about Dad's dismal situation and asked if she had a walking cane that she could spare. The woman told her that she could not help her, but that if Irmgard would climb up the stairs to the second floor, she could see if the old gentleman who had lived there had left a walking cane. Irmgard went up the stairs and found what she was looking for. She selected one that she thought might be useful to Dad and came down again to thank the woman for it. The cane helped Dad a lot, and he was even able to walk a little faster. (This cane served him for many years after the war.)

By late afternoon they returned to the harbor halls. When Mom saw Dad, she cried her heart out. Oh how happy she was that we were once again together. Mom told Irmgard and Lieschen many times that the angel of God must have been with them. In their thankfulness they offered many a sincere prayer to God who is always near when we need Him most. But we still needed Him, for our journey of escaping the horrors of that war was far from over.

The next day, after the waves of emotions had calmed a bit, Mom told Irmgard and Lieschen that they should go to the local Brownshirt's headquarters and ask for a place to live, since it was obvious that we could not stay in the harbor halls for too long. These were only a reception place for the refugees that came in daily by the hundreds and thousands. So my sisters went looking for the Nazi headquarters. En route Lieschen started to cry again, and the more she cried, the more Irmgard got mad at her. "This is no time for crying," she scolded her. But not even that made Lieschen stop crying.

Suddenly two officers stood in front of them and asked why she was crying. One of the officers was in an army uniform, although his left arm was missing; the other wore a navy uniform. Irmgard told them that her sister was simply at the end of her rope and that the stress of the war was too much for her. She also mentioned to them that they were on their way to the Nazi headquarters to find a place to stay since we had to get out of the harbor halls. After listening to Irmgard explain the situation, the one-armed officer told them that he had just what they were looking for, namely an empty apartment. Then he asked my sisters to come along and have a look at the place. So they went along. After they saw the apartment, the army officer suggested that they go get the lodging permit from the Nazi headquarters and then move in.

The girls had no problem finding the dreaded building since all the people they asked for directions seemed to know where the place was. But to get the lodging permit turned into a real problem. When they entered the plush office, a corpulent Brownshirt bigwig shouted at them to tell him what they wanted. Irmgard told him that they had come to request a lodging permit so they could move from the harbor halls into an apartment. Then she mentioned that we had been offered a place already, which turned out to be the wrong thing to do. You never tell a superior being like that that you have already solved the matter that he is in charge of. "Who do you think you are?" he shouted at them in a very angry voice. "It is my job to find lodging for refugees and nobody else's business. Where would things get if everybody did as they pleased!"

With that he refused to give them a lodging permit. Irmgard asked him once more to be so kind and give her the permit. But in a stern and cold voice, he told her that for him the matter was already settled and that they should get out of his office before he lost his temper. Then Irmgard said to him that she too considered the matter settled—he should keep his lodging permit, for we would move into the apartment even without his permission! As they went out the door, Irmgard turned and mentioned in passing that in a few short days the Russians would be here for sure and then there would no longer be a need for a lodging permit anymore. And with that they left and went back to the harbor hall.

When they told Mom and Dad the news about the apartment and what had happened at the Nazi office, Dad told her that she would get us into deep trouble for not showing respect to that Nazi bigwig. But regardless of what could happen to us, we grabbed our few belongings and vacated the spot that for two days had given us some badly needed rest. As soon as we picked up our blanket rolls and rucksacks to leave, another refugee family hastily took our spot. The demand for shelter was so great. The refugees who were staying in these corrugated metal harbor storage halls came from all over the Eastern provinces of Germany, but mostly from East Prussia. And since a continuing stream of refugees was arriving daily, it was not always easy to find a place in the overcrowded halls.

To say the least, we were more than happy to get out of there, even if that meant we could get in trouble with the feared and dreaded Nazis. Since these were such chaotic days, my parents counted on it that the Nazis had more important things to do than locating us. When we arrived at the large, three-storied house, my parents realized that this had been a ritzy neighborhood and wondered what we were doing there as poor refugees. But Irmgard rang one of the doorbells and the friendly army officer opened the door and let us in. Then he showed us the apartment on the second floor, which had four rooms plus a kitchen, bath, spacious passageway, and balcony. These were amenities common folks in the old country could only dream of.

After he had shown us around, he gave the key to my parents and told them that we should just make ourselves comfortable and feel at home. But just then the doorbell rang and the landlady of the house was at the door. And since she talked in a rather loud voice, we could clearly hear what she told the army officer who had opened the door. She demanded that he throw us out immediately for this was a nice house and not an asylum for dirty refugees. He then reminded her that his niece had handed the apartment over to him and he could do with it as he pleased, and with that he closed the door on her. We moved into the three rooms and quickly figured out that the niece's husband must have been a Nazi bigwig.

After the officer had gone to his room, as all adventurous boys do, I went through our rooms and closets to see if anything of interest had been left behind. In one of the closets I found a number of Nazi uniforms as well as other Nazi stuff, and in a drawer I found a music box that played familiar Nazi songs. When my father heard the music, he entered the room and told me to shut it off. Then I showed him what I had found. He immediately took the music box away from me and asked my older sisters to find a box for the uniforms. They found a cardboard box and put all the Nazi stuff into it. Then, under cover of darkness, my dad disposed of this "deadly" parcel far from where we were staying. Dad told us that if the Russians were to find us in an apartment with all those Nazi uniforms and things they would shoot us on the spot. And that is exactly what happened to my mom's brother, Uncle Otto Völzke. He had taken in refugees and other people who were in need of a place to stay and someone had hid a Nazi uniform in the attic. When the Poles who came with the Russian army found the uniform in his attic, they did not bother to find out if he was a Nazi or not. They just dragged Uncle Otto out of his house and clubbed him to death.

In the late afternoon the army officer asked Mom if she would be willing to cook supper. He motioned to the balcony and said that there was a dried side of beef and in the kitchen she would find some potatoes as well as carrots and onions to make a good beef soup. So Mom and the girls got busy in the kitchen, and in a little while some mouthwatering smells filled the apartment. We had not enjoyed too many hot meals since leaving our home in Stolp. The smells made us all the more hungry for a good meal. When the soup was ready, we thanked God many times for such a nourishing meal.

The army officer and his friend ate with us too, and if their healthy appetites were an indicator of how they rated Mom's cooking, they must have liked it very much. After supper Dad spoke with the officers. He told them where we came from and what we had suffered so far. He told them too how Irmgard and Lieschen had searched for him to get him out of the Volkssturm barracks. The army officer then told him that he and his friend would be leaving Danzig that night by submarine. The navy officer assured Dad that he would gladly take us all along, but civilians were not allowed on the submarine. Taking his army friend, who actually had been ordered to stay behind with his unit to defend Danzig, was quite risky, but he could not let his best friend down. They told us they would be gone by morning.

After breakfast my older sisters went looking for groceries. But to their utter surprise and dismay, no store was willing to take their Pomeranian food coupons. And since we did not have any others, they came back empty-handed. Looking for groceries could be quite a risky business since the ground support fighters were continually dropping splinter-bombs and shot with their cannons at every moving thing, so we were most happy that they simply arrived back home, even though they didn't have any food.

Even though we were quite low on food we were not starving yet. For dinner Mom prepared another excellent meal thanks to the dried beef and spuds the former occupants had left behind. Soon after dinner the doorbell rang. Now my parents and older sisters got really nervous. Naturally they feared that the Nazis had located us and would take us all to the concentration camp or simply kill us. In one of the small towns we had come through some time ago, we had seen three or four soldiers hanging by the neck from a tree. Perhaps this would be our end too.

When Mom, after mustering all her courage, opened the apartment door, there stood an army officer and from behind him peeped the landlady. He turned out to be the quartermaster for a repair company and was looking for lodging for his soldiers. They had been pulled out from the frontline to get some badly needed rest, and he wanted to know if she would be willing to take some of his boys in. My mother told him that we would gladly share the apartment with some of his soldiers. Since the place had four rooms, she said we could live in one and he could have the other three. When the landlady heard that, she almost flipped out. From behind the officer she hollered that we had small kids and grownup girls and could not possibly sleep all in one room together, but she made it very clear that no soldiers were allowed in her house.

It seemed that the officer had had enough. He turned to the landlady and in a voice that rang with authority and tolerated no opposition said, "Take a look at this refugee lady. She has lost everything, yet she has sympathy for my soldiers, while you show absolutely no sympathy at all. Therefore, I will requisite your house and we are going to set up our office in your apartment!"

When she heard this, her face turned as white as a sheet, and since she knew that the officer had the powers to do that, she left for her apartment. The field kitchen as well as some other army vehicles soon appeared in the backyard and two soldiers came to our apartment to stay with us. Mom showed them one of the bedrooms and told them that they should make themselves comfortable and feel at home. After a little while the officer came back and thanked Mom for the kindness she had shown to his soldiers. My father stayed in bed trying to regain his strength.

The next day the officer sent word through the two soldiers that we could get our food from their field kitchen. This sounded almost too good to be true since we were unable to buy any groceries and our food stuffs had dwindled down to some old bread. As with Elijah in Bible days, God sent the soldiers, in place of ravens, to feed us. Thank God for His providence and care.

One early evening after we had been living in the apartment about five days, we heard a low grumble in the distant western sky and knew instantly that it came from the bombers. In the fading rays of the sunset, I started to count them but did not get too far when suddenly from the first planes we saw some lights appearing that seemed to float in the air. These lights were called *Tannenbäume* (Christmas tree) in German and were released by the Pathfinder planes to show the bombers where to drop their deadly load. That particular evening the bombers leveled the harbor storage halls in which we had stayed only a few short days ago. In His mercy God had placed us in the apartment and saved us from perishing with all the other refugees. I have often wondered why our merciful Father spread His wings over us. We were certainly not more deserving of His protection and care than the other refugees, but He clearly had a plan for us.

All night long we could see the reflection of the burning harbor halls in the sky, and knowing that all those refugees had perished there, my parents and older sisters cried bitterly. Renate and I were too young to understand the severity of what happened that night.

Two days after the air raid on the harbor storage halls, it was our turn. Across from our backyard, a huge pile of empty gasoline drums were stored, and I can imagine that when the reconnaissance planes came back and the pictures were analyzed, the air force decided that the pile of drums was worth another air raid. When the sirens sounded, we all ran to the basement of the house, which had been converted into a bomb shelter. In anticipation of the raid, the soldiers left and moved their vehicles from the backyard to the street as well as to other streets to try avoid big losses. After that some of them came to the bomb shelter too. With each exploding bomb, the house shook and seemed to shift on its foundation—every second we feared that the house would collapse on us and bury us all alive. Those were horrible moments. Nobody was really sure how long the explosions and tremors lasted. It seemed as if the whole earth was shaking just like in an earthquake.

In the haste to get to the bomb shelter, Irmgard had lost one of her shoes upstairs. After the bombing had ceased somewhat, she wanted to go and retrieve her shoe, so one of the soldiers who had stayed with us accompanied her. When they got to the apartment they smelled smoke, so they climbed to the third story and found it already in flames. After finding her shoe, they rushed down again to the relative safety of the bomb shelter. Irmgard told us that all the windows had been smashed and the window crosses had been sucked out of the frames and were lying on the street and the house was on fire. Further, all the other houses around us were destroyed and burning. It seemed as if the whole neighborhood was one inferno. While Irmgard and the soldier were explaining what they had seen, a soldier who had been sent by the quartermaster showed up and whispered to Dad that we should get ready if we wanted to come along with them. Although the army was not permitted to take civilians along in their vehicles, the kind officer went against these orders to help us out.

Dad realized that this was our only chance to get out of Danzig, which was clearly burning to the ground. He told the soldier we would be ready in a minute or two. Since there were other people with us in the bomb shelter and this was a secret offer of assistance, Dad whispered to Irmgard and Lieschen that they should go and try to get our few belongings out of the burning house. My sisters went up to the apartment, fetched our blanket rolls as well as the rucksack with the dried bread, grabbed a few other things, and took them straight to the waiting army vehicles.

After that they came for us, but a burly Nazi blocked their way down to the apartment bomb shelter. He asked them where they were going. Irmgard told him that they were on their way to meet their parents in the bomb shelter. He ordered them not to move from the spot, and told them they were needed to get a big fire under control. He was looking for more people in other bomb shelters on our street and would be back right away. He told them that if they moved or ran away he would shoot them. With that he left and went looking for more people.

My sisters stood on the street with the burning buildings and piles of rubble everywhere. Total chaos surrounding them, and they felt that they had nothing to lose. When the Nazi disappeared in another bomb shelter, my sisters ran to our bomb shelter to get us. They quickly helped Dad up the stairs. Mom and I followed them, and the soldier who had stayed with us carried Renate and led the way to the waiting army vehicles. Since nobody was to know that the army was transporting us, they had to be careful not to arouse any suspicion. Our family was stowed away in one vehicle, and as soon as we jumped in, the soldiers drove off.

It was very slow going. All the bridges had been destroyed and the whole city seemed to be ablaze. Although the soldier leading the convoy of vehicles had been born and raised in the city, he found it difficult to find a way out of the city. The convoy had to turn around several times in order not to burn the tires since the asphalt of the street was on fire. Of course, turning around on those narrow streets was not an easy task for the army vehicles. After many hours, in fact it was morning, we finally made it out of Danzig.

The convoy stopped briefly in a small village under cover of the broad branches of some trees in a cemetery to avoid detection by the ground support fighter aircrafts that were almost constantly overhead. After only a few moments the convoy left again to find a larger forest to hide in and get away from the *Jabos*, as the ground support fighters were called in German. By now the Russian artillery were also firing, trying to destroy the road and those who used it.

As soon as the convoy leader found a large forest, he ordered the vehicles to disperse in the woods. We found that the woods were full of other soldiers as well as all kinds of army vehicles and countless refugees. The place was called *Krakau Forest*. As soon as our convoy had dispersed in the woods, the officer in charge ordered his soldiers to dig in. So they started to dig short trenches with small shelters at the end of the trenches. The shelters consisted of a hole in the ground that was covered with logs that were hastily cut in the surrounding pine forest and a pile of sand from the dunes covered up the wooden ceiling. Within minutes of us crawling into the shelter, the bombardment started. It lasted for three hours, and Irmgard confided in me many years after the war that she did not think we would make it out alive.

In the afternoon when the air raid finally ceased, the soldiers told us that we should go to the field kitchen and get a hot meal. In order to get to the field kitchen, we had to cross a large clearing. My older sisters helped Dad while Mother, Renate, and I followed behind them. We had made it about two-thirds of the way across the clearing when a *Jabo* came low over the treetops. Seeing us in the open, he immediately started shooting at us. My sisters tried to hurry poor Dad along, and we ran for the cover of the forest. Lucky for us, the pilot was not good at aiming at moving targets. By the time we reached the safety of the pines, he had turned around and was coming back to give it another try. Fortunately, he couldn't see us in the woods, and no one was injured by his random shooting.

We had no problem finding the field kitchen. All we had to do was follow our noses since the light breeze that wafted through the woods brought the delicious aroma of rice-and-beef stew to our nostrils. There were six of us with only one dish and spoon, but we gladly shared with each other. Since the stew was a little on the lean side, which is to say that it was a bit thin, we did not even need a spoon to eat it. We simply drank it. After we had eaten, these kindhearted soldiers told us to hang around until supper was served. They assured us that there was enough for us too. We decided to stay near the field kitchen instead of chancing a run across the clearing.

We made our way a short distance from the field kitchen to a shelter that had been prepared for a few horses. Dad told us not to get too close to them since they might kick when disturbed by the noise of the detonating bombs. But Mom, Irmgard, Renate, and I entered the shelter, staying as far away as possible from the tail end of the horses. Dad sat down near the shelter and leaned against the big trunk of a pine tree while Lieschen stood beside another tree. Suddenly a *Jabo* came zooming over the treetops and released its bombs, which exploded close by. Dad shouted to Lieschen to get down on the ground when we heard a splinter hit a tree, the very tree that Lieschen had seconds before stood beside. At the same time we heard Dad holler that he had been hit in the shoulder.

Mom and Irmgard rushed over to Dad to see what damage the splinter had caused to Dad's arm. When I saw the blood on Dad's hand, I, as well as Renate, started to cry, which added to the already existing confusion. Fortunately, the splinter had lost most of its force because it first hit the tree. When it hit Dad's arm, it penetrated the muscles but did not destroy the bone. In all likelihood, the padding of the shirt sleeves as well as coat sleeves also helped to somewhat deaden the velocity of the splinter. We were most thankful that our loving heavenly Father had once again prevented the worst from happening, namely Dad losing his entire arm. We were also thankful Lieschen had responded to Dad's warning and thrown herself on the ground before the splinter had hit the tree. If she hadn't, she would have probably been killed.

Isn't it wonderful to know that God is watching over us, spreading His mighty wings out in love to protect us in peaceful and perilous days? We certainly were thankful to know that He cared for us as we faced those days of uncertainty and turmoil.

As usual, Irmgard sprung to action at the first sign of the emergency. She took her scarf and folded it into a sling, which she then put around Dad's neck. After that she took his arm and gently put it into the sling for support. One of the soldiers who had been in our vicinity came over and had a look at Dad's wound. He then called for a medic, but no one came. After some time, they found one, and he examined Dad's wounded arm. He then told Dad that he needed to see a doctor. As he left, Irmgard and Dad followed him. When they finally found the doctor, he told Dad he had no more medicine or tranquilizers to treat him with. The only thing he still had were paper bandages. Dad told him to just remove the splinter and treat the wound. However, the doctor had some objections to Dad's suggestion. But since the splinter had to be removed, the doctor had no other choice.

The doctor told Dad to sit down on the forest floor and lean against a tree trunk. Then the medic took the wounded arm and held it while Irmgard took hold of the other arm. Since Irmgard had used coats and shirts to stop the bleeding, the doctor first removed the clothes from the wound. Then he cut the splinter out with a scalpel. Irmgard did not see much of the operation since her eyes were constantly filled with tears knowing that Dad was in so much pain. The splinter was as long as a finger and bent to form a triangle. After the operation, the doctor said it was a miracle Dad had not lost his arm. Once he was finished, he put a pressure bandage on the wound to stop the bleeding and bandaged everything with paper bandages. After that the doctor gave Dad an info card on which he wrote the particulars about Dad's injury, where and when he had received the wound and what care had been administered. Then he fastened the card around Dad's neck.

Before the doctor left, he told Dad that he should go to the next army field hospital to get further treatment. He definitely needed a tetanus shot. If he didn't get the injection, he would be a dead man in three days. Irmgard and Dad slowly made their way back to the trenches where the rest of us had retreated after Dad got wounded. A soldier brought us supper. Toward evening as it was getting dark we heard the drone of the on-coming bombers again. First there were the "Pathfinder" planes that dropped the marker lights. After that came the bombers with their deadly loads. And even though we were some distance away from where the bombs were dropped, it seemed as if all hell broke loose. After the raid was over, we tried to get some sleep.

In the morning when we woke up, we noticed that one of the sides of the trench in which we had slept had caved in and nearly buried us. While we ate our breakfast, the officer in charge of the soldiers came and talked to Dad. He told him that they had received orders to stay here and get ready to help defend Danzig. Therefore, he thought it would be best for us to go to a place where the navy was helping refugees escape the battle. Besides, Dad needed to see a doctor and get his tetanus shot. However, we did not leave that day. In fact, we stayed there three more days. My sisters went with Dad to locate the army field hospital, but they came back looking rather discouraged. On the morning of the fourth day, we shouldered our bedrolls and our few other belongings and started off in the direction the soldiers had given us to find the field hospital. Before we left, our friendly hosts had seen to it that our dwindling supply of food had been replenished.

Soon we found a forest road with lots of refugees all walking in the direction we were told the field hospital was located, so we followed them. After an hour or so, we suddenly found ourselves on a riverbank with no bridge across the water. A small ferry took the refugees to the other side. Most of the time it was overloaded since everybody wanted to get across immediately. While walking through the forest, we had only the occasional air attack, but now that there was a large crowd standing in line waiting for the ferry, an almost endless stream of attacks ensued trying to sink the little ferry that was the lifeline for the refugees. As soon as we heard the fighters screaming down toward the ferry, shooting wildly with cannons and machine guns, we ran to some old army vehicles that had been abandoned at the edge of the forest and crawled under an armored personnel carrier for safety. Luckily for the refugees on the ferry, the airplane pilot was a poor shot, and he missed his target repeatedly. But as soon as one plane was gone, another one came screaming down with fiery flashes from the muzzles as the guns and cannons fired at anything moving.

We felt it was imperative that we reach the army field hospital, so we waited for a lull in the air attacks. The German antiaircraft batteries stationed around the ferry were doing their best to make life hard for the daring pilots. This surely was a battle for survival, however, not of the fittest, but of the more skilled! Again a fighter dove toward the ferry, shooting with all its barrels. The Germans answered back, and this time they hit their mark. As I watched this deadly shootout, I suddenly noticed black smoke erupt from the motor of the airplane and soon the pilot bailed out of the burning aircraft. While he floated toward the ground, his fighter spun toward earth and exploded upon impact. This hit brought about a brief lull in the action. Dad seized the moment and hollered for us to run to the ferry. Everyone pushed and shoved to get on board, and our family was separated in the chaos. Mom, Dad, and Renate got on, and before we knew it, the operator started for the other shore. My older sisters and I had to wait for his return.

Before they were even close to the other shore, another fighter appeared and began shooting at the ferry. The bullets hit the water, sending water spraying. The bullets got closer and closer to the ferry. People started screaming for fear they would soon be killed. But God once again spread His wings over our family so that the deadly hail of bullets missed the ferry and its passengers. The ferry operator ran the ferry onto the shallow riverbank, and everyone rushed ashore and sought cover since the next fighter was bearing down on them. Once again the Germans scored a hit, and the already diving plane fell to the ground and burst into flames.

Again there was a lull in the attack. The ferry operator quickly made his way across the river and picked the rest of us up. But before we had made it across the river, another fighter dove toward us and shot at the ferry. Again the trail of bullets hit the water and raced toward the ferry. Everyone screamed and huddled together in fear. However, the ferry operator managed to steer his craft to shore unharmed. As soon as we were on shore, we ran for the cover of the trees. In short order we found Mom and Dad and Renate. They had waited for us in a ditch beside the road.

We followed the country road and the stream of refugees. Before long we came to a place that had been bombed some nights before. It had been a pine forest, but the explosions had left the forest looking like a bunch of splintered matchsticks. It was an eerie sight, for there was not a single tree standing in all the forest. Besides, the forest had been full of refugees, who now lay dead on what used to be the forest floor. I turned to Irmgard and asked, "Are all these people dead?" It was a very sad and disturbing sight. As we continued on that road, we walked past a former forest clearing that was filled with destroyed and overturned army vehicles, but there were no corpses among them. Dad told me that it had been a dump for unusable vehicles. We wondered if this could have been the reason for the bombardment.

After a short walk we arrived at the village of Bohnensack, or what was left of it. The incendiary bombs that had been dropped had set the whole village ablaze. Everywhere one looked lay heaps of bodies. Some were burned; others were wounded. My older sisters took Renate and me and tried to cover our heads with their scarfs so that we wouldn't see the death and destruction, but it was too late. The horrible, appalling, gruesome sight was forever etched in my memory.

The village of Bohnensack lay in the Weichsel River delta and was located on one of the Weichsel channels that emptied into the Baltic Sea. When we got to the pier, there were two navy vessels loading refugees. We did not know where they would take us to, but we boarded the *flak* boats, as they were called in German on account of the many antiaircraft gun turrets they had. As the refugees boarded the vessels, burly military police combed the crowd looking for men to help fight the lost war. One of these fellows saw that Dad had a card hanging around his neck and came over to inspect the card. When he read the message that Dad needed immediate medical attention, he told him to board the vessel. But Dad said he would not go without his family, so he motioned us to board as well. The only place for us on the boat was right under a four-barreled antiaircraft gun tower. And since beggars can't be choosers, we made ourselves comfortable right under that tower. As soon as the two navy vessels were loaded to the brim with refugees, the vessels headed out to sea.

Soon after entering the waters of the Baltic Sea, several Russian bombers appeared and started dropping their bombs. The antiaircraft guns made a hellish noise as they tried to shoot the bombers down. Renate was scared to death and started weeping and hollering at the top of her lungs. After all, she was only six years old. Mom took her on her lap and put her arms around her to comfort her, but nothing seemed to help. When someone put a newspaper over her head, she calmed down somewhat. But she never really recovered from this nerve-racking experience in later life.

Some of the bombs fell rather close to our ship. When they hit the water, great fountains gushed skyward. And even though the sailors were feeding the four-barreled gun on the tower like mad, they did not shoot any of the bombers down. We watched the tracer bullets as they streaked up toward them, but the bombers kept stolidly on their course. Praise God this was the only incident on that voyage. After some hours we arrived at the fishing port of Hela, which was situated at the very end of the Hela peninsula. Since it was almost evening, we had to find some shelter for the night. After a short search, my older sisters found some room in a chicken coop close to the village church. They also found a broom to clean the hen house from all the dirt that had been left behind by the former feathered occupants, who seemed to have vanished before we showed up, perhaps to some warm little oven to help nourish their owners. To say the least, this turned out to be a big mistake. After we had settled in, we soon found out that this place was heavily infested with hungry fleas. Needless to say, after the fleas started to "dine" on us, we scratched without ceasing all night. Should you ever have the desire to find out how the Egyptian plague of lice must have felt to those people of old, go and stay one night in a chicken coop infested with fleas!

As you can imagine, we did not get much sleep that night and were more than glad when a new day started to dawn. We speedily gathered our few belongings together and went looking for another shelter. Since the village church was close by, we thought of staying there, but the church was already overcrowded with refugees. By now Dad's wound was giving him a lot of pain, so we decided to stay outside the church while Dad and Irmgard tried to locate an army hospital. After only a short search, they found the place. The medic on duty read Dad's note that he still had hanging around his neck and went to find the doctor. When the doctor read what day Dad had been wounded, he wondered how he was still alive without having been given a tetanus shot. He then regretfully told Dad that he did not have any tetanus injection for him either. However, he said he was willing to look at the wound and do whatever he could to help him.

The doctor took off the bandages and inspected the wound. Irmgard almost passed out when she saw the blackened, rotting flesh around the wound. Unfortunately, the doctor did not have any anesthetic drugs to numb the pain while cleaning the wound, so Dad would just have to bear the pain. The doctor set to work cleaning the wound and putting another pressure bandage on. Then he wrote a new note, put it around Dad's neck, and told them to see if they could get him on one of the hospital ships anchored outside the harbor.

Upon leaving the hospital, they found the hospital ship and told them what the doctor had said. They were informed that the hospital ships only admitted wounded soldiers. Besides, they did not allow family members to come on board. Dad and Irmgard returned to the church where we had been waiting and told us about their morning activities. Since we would need a shelter for the coming night, Lieschen and Irmgard headed out to look for something better than we had the night before. While they were gone, I asked permission from my parents to go down to the harbor. I was told not to stay too long or get lost.

When I got to the harbor, I found lots of dead fish, a direct result of the bombs that had been dropped in the sea. When a bomb explodes in the water, it destroys the swim bladder in the fish that are nearby, killing them instantly. The dead fish then floated to the surface of the sea and washed ashore. For many of the refugees, these fish became their lifeline since food was scarce and hard to find. I even saw some people fighting over the dead fish. Hunger and greed seem to bring out the worst in people, especially when they are desperate.

Remembering my parents' directive to not stay too long down by the harbor, I headed back to the church. I came back right on time since Irmgard was about to come and look for me. My sisters had found us a place to stay, but they were in a hurry to get there before someone else claimed the spot. The room was in an old fisherman's hut. It was quite dirty, but hopefully it didn't have fleas. As soon as we had moved in, other refugees came looking for a shelter. But since the room was very small, we could not accommodate them. The whole village was filled with refugees and confusion seemed to prevail. After we ate, Mom mentioned to my older sisters that we would soon need more bread and other food items. So off they went in search of supplies.

After quite some time they came back with a few loaves of bread and some cheese that they secured on the black market, since our Pomeranian food stamps, as already mentioned earlier, were not accepted in the stores. How thankful we all were that God had opened a door for us to get some food. In the evening we settled down for the night on the floor beside the inside wall of the room. Since the room was not heated, it was rather chilly. We covered up with our blankets and huddled close together to preserve warmth. After only a few hours of sleep, the sirens woke us up and we rushed to the nearest bomb shelter. Lucky for us, these were only a few Russian bombers and not the formidable American bombers that could level a place like Hela in one run. After a dozen or so explosions, the sirens sounded again, and we went back to our shelter.

The next morning we heard that most of the bombs had fallen into the sea and the damage was rather minimal. We remained in Hela a few days, not knowing how to leave or where to go. The Russian bombers and some other fighter planes kept us hopping in and out of the bomb shelter, letting us know that soon they would be here for good. With so many displaced persons coming and going, all sorts of rumors were on the wing. The morning of Good Friday, 1945, my sisters came home with a rumor that there were small boats at some piers a short distance away from the fishing harbor of Hela that were taking refugees out to old freighters that would take them to Denmark. This sounded too good to be true. At that time Denmark was one of the few places that could be considered a safe haven for refugees since it was occupied by the German military and far away from the Russians who, out of all the allied forces, committed deplorable atrocities on the innocent and defenseless civilians.

To find out the truth, Dad suggested that Lieschen and Irmgard go to the pier and find out more about the matter. Soon after the girls had left, they returned out of breath. They told us to pack our bags and hurry to the pier— the rumor was true! The military was already loading refugees onto the waiting freighters. As soon as our few things had been packed and the blankets rolled up, we shouldered our rucksacks with the precious foodstuffs and hurried to the pier.

By now most other refugees had found out that the freighters anchored some distance from shore were a means of escape. The large crowd pushed and shoved in an effort to get through the pier gates, which were manned by sailors and armed military police. Once we were in the crowd, we were shoved along in the flow of humanity making its way to the pier. At the gate the sailors separated the refugees. Only women with children and old men were allowed to go on the pier proper, from which tugboats and other small vessels took the people over to the waiting freighters. The military police scoured the crowd for men and older boys who they could recruit to prolong the fighting. And no tearful pleading by mothers who did not want to be separated from their sons or screaming by wives who did not want to lose their husbands helped. How these hardened men could take crying schoolboys away from their mothers or feeble, old men from their wives when everybody knew the war was lost is beyond anyone's understanding.

We wondered what would happen to Dad and if he would be allowed to board with us or not. When we got to the gates, one of the sailors saw the note that Dad was wearing around his neck and asked him to go through. Dad told him that he had his family with him and asked that we be allowed to accompany him. When the sailor saw my older sisters, he indicated that they could not go along. Perhaps Dad remembered what Abram did in Egypt, how he told the Egyptians that his wife Sarai was his sister for fear that they would kill him and take her as a bride, but Dad thought fast and told the sailor and military officer who had come to inspect Dad's medical note that Renate was Lieschen's child and I was Irmgard's son. The sailor's mouth momentarily dropped open in surprise, but when he looked at my older sisters, who held Renate and me close in their arms, he smiled and let us all go through. Mom had tears in her eyes. We were still all together!

We were told to hurry. Since it was quite foggy no bombers or fighters were in the air to harass or disturb the loading process; however, the officials wanted to load the freighters as fast as possible so that the convoy could slip away in the fog. When we got to the freighter, only the sick or very young were heaved on board by the windlass; everybody else had to crawl up the wall by way of rope ladders. Dad and Renate, as well as many others, were put in a huge net and heaved on board. The rest of our family and most of the refugees came up the hard way. I'll be honest with you, most of us were rather frightened to climb up that steep and swinging rope ladder. After all, there was always the possibility that one might slip and fall into the sea and drown.

When we reached the railing after our harrowing climb, sailors helped us get on deck. We were then quickly ushered below deck via stairs in the hold doors. As we were descending the ladder into the hold, Dad found us and told us not to go all the way down to the bottom. So we looked for a place on the second level below deck. The first level was reserved for the Nazi bigwigs. In case of a submarine attack, they would have the best chance of getting out of the sinking ship. That's why Dad wanted to be as close to the top deck as possible. We decided to set up camp close to the ladder we had just come down. Old mattresses had been put on the floor for people to rest and sleep on. We found a spot just big enough for the six of us, and we spread out our bedrolls to signal that the place was occupied.

At this point, our most valuable earthly possession was the rucksack with our food, which we guarded at all times, since stealing was looked upon as no big thing since it was a method of survival. We quickly discovered that the mattresses were infested with fleas and lice and bed bugs. But then again, this was the life one led as a refugee. Cleanliness was not something we were privileged enough to enjoy. Sometimes days passed before we could even wash our face and hands. And washing your whole body was a luxury very few refugees enjoyed. All of this filth made for a perfect environment for the insects to thrive in.

After the Orundi, as the freighter was named, was loaded to the brim with refugees (6,000 of them, plus some navy staff as well as fleeing Nazis), we set out. By now the fog had lifted somewhat, so one was able to see the shadowy outlines of the other vessels as well as the destroyers that escorted our convoy for protection. As soon as I felt that the vessel was moving, I wanted to go on deck to see what was going on out there. But my parents did not allow me to go alone, so Irmgard came along. When we arrived on deck, I looked back and noticed that Lieschen and Renate had followed us. The deck was crowded with other refugees who wanted to witness our departure from Hela. I tried to climb up to the commando bridge but was told that only the sailors were permitted there. Their duty was to look out for signs of danger since we were in submarine infested waters.

After a short time one of my sisters needed a washroom, so we started looking around for one. There did not seem to be any in the hold area, so we figured they must be on deck. And sure enough they were. They had been constructed by the railing, and all of the waste was continuously flushed overboard. The toilets could accommodate as many as fifteen people at the same time, but they were totally void of any comfort or privacy. In fact, there were not even doors at the sides where one entered these lofty "thrones." One had to sit on a rail just like the chickens in a coop and could chat with your neighbors who shared the rail with you. Irmgard told me later that she did not go to the bathroom for two days and after that only in the dark!

The whole voyage to Copenhagen lasted almost three days, and in all that time we did not get any food. The food on board the ship was reserved for the Nazis on the first level. This elite lot had, even now when everybody else was almost starving, so much to eat that they would cut the crust off their bread and throw it away. How do I know that? Some other boys my age, which I had met while walking around in the hold where we all stayed, and I begged the sailors for those scraps of bread after they delivered the food to the Nazi officials on the deck above us. Like hungry vultures, we waited for them every mealtime, and when they came back with the garbage, we gulped down the food scraps. If it were not for the bread and cheese my sisters bought for us on the black market in Hela, this trip would have turned into a voyage of starvation. But because of God's care, we had something to eat and did not have to go hungry.

We soon got used to the noise of the ship's engine and were able to catch some sleep, and yes, slowly one learned to tolerate the little insects that bit us in the night. Naturally, the "hunt" for all those little vermin went on all day. Mother and my sisters combed their long hair more than usual to look for the nasty lice that lived near their scalp. Mother regularly searched our clothes, especially our shirts and underwear, for lice and bedbugs. To say the least, there was never a dull moment in the ordinary life of the poor refugees.

Toward late afternoon of the second day into our voyage, when we were in the Bay of Pomerania, the ship's engine abruptly slowed down and came almost to a standstill. At the same time, we felt the vessel lean over toward port until it was at a very steep and dangerous angle. This threw everyone into a panic. Those who had been standing either jumped or fell down to the floor or on the mattresses. The more the vessel leaned, the more people slid and rolled, making the already existing chaos only worse. The screams of those injured in the process and by others who feared for their lives was deafening. Those closest to the stairs tried to climb up and get out of the hold, but only those who were strong and agile succeeded. Naturally, chaos also reigned on the level above us. It was good to see that in an unexpected situation all people become equal in a matter of seconds. All fear losing their lives and all try to preserve it.

After some fearful moments, or were they perhaps hours, the vessel slowly righted itself again, and now the despised Nazis came up on deck in droves. Once righted the imminent danger seemed to be over, at least, that's what we all hoped. Everybody began asking what had happened, and we soon learned the answer. Our vessel had been attacked by a submarine. I am sure that when the captain of the Russian submarine looked through his periscope and saw the rather slow moving convoy with only a few escort vessels, which were plying their course through the calm waters of the Baltic Sea, like lame ducks on a pond, he anticipated an easy turkey shoot. However, it did not turn out that way.

I know that the Captain of the Lord's host stood beside the sailors on the commando bridge of our vessel and held the ship in His hands and kept it upright in this dangerous situation. The news spread like wildfire that one of the crewmen on watch, while scanning the sea with his binoculars for signs of danger, had suddenly noticed a line of bubbles in the sea that was fast approaching our vessel. He immediately shouted the alarm. Since most torpedoes in the Second World War were propelled by compressed air, many times the telltale line of bubbles that rose to the surface of the sea after the torpedo had been fired gave these deadly *eels*, as they were commonly called in German, away and helped save lives. When my parents heard the news, they sent a prayer of thanks to heaven for God's protection. For the few lifeboats and rafts that were on the deck of the freighter were not nearly enough to even save half of the 6,000 souls on board.

Oh friend, be thankful for every day the Lord grants you, and be happy in the certain knowledge that you can rest safe and secure under His mighty wings no matter what difficult life situations you may be facing. Regardless of how dark and dreary the storm clouds may look, He will find a way of escape! Jesus, who gave His precious life to secure eternal life for us, loves us and understands our infirmities and shortcomings. He will never give up on us. Regrettably and ironically, only our own deliberate choosing will sever the lifeline with our loving Lord. Just when life seems utterly hopeless, He is closest to us. Do you remember the thief on the cross? His situation seemed hopeless, but Jesus provided a way of escape for him. When, in his utter hopelessness, he turned to Jesus, he immediately received the assurance that he would be with Christ in heaven someday. What an inspiring story that is! It has certainly given me tremendous hope and strength, especially in life's dreariest and darkest moments.

God's providence was even more evident when we heard the rest of the story. As soon as the watchman gave the alarm, two things happened. First the naval captain shouted the order to turn to port, and the helmsman turned the wheel hard and harder toward port. This caused the vessel to lean over until we all thought it would keel over. The second order was to cut the engine in order to slow down the speed of the vessel. These maneuvers were successful and the torpedo missed its target. Sometimes I have wondered what went through the minds of the men on the commando bridge. Did they think only of themselves and perhaps their loved ones, which they might never see again, or did they perhaps feel a responsibility toward the thousands of refugees below deck that would perish in the icy waters of the Baltic Sea if the torpedo hit? I like to think that they also thought of us as they shouted out orders and tried their best to save the ship. The submarine luckily only fired that one shot.

Irmgard, myself, and Lieschen (From left to right) in the summer of 1955.

Everyone on board breathed a sigh of relief after the ordeal was over. After the incident, a new rule was made, and we were only permitted on deck to use the toilets. Otherwise we had to stay in our quarters below. Praise God the rest of the voyage went smoothly without any further disturbance. Not even the ever present warplanes showed themselves out over the sea. If it were not for the lack of food or the uncertainty that was still before us, one could perhaps have even enjoyed this trip across the Baltic Sea.

Late Easter Sunday we finally arrived in Copenhagen. We were very happy to see land again. Our vessel was moored at a pier in the harbor and that was all that happened that evening. Naturally, we all hoped we could leave the ship immediately. Instead we were still detained all day Monday. Under no circumstances were we permitted to leave the vessel. To show that the officials meant business, they placed armed soldiers on the pier to guard the ship. The worst, however, was that nobody brought us any food. It seemed that the officials thought refugees did not get hungry.

Finally, on Tuesday, April 4, 1945, nearly a month after we had fled from our home in the quiet town of Stolp, army trucks came to the pier to take us to a refugee camp somewhere in Copenhagen. Even though the friendly sailors assured us that all would be able to leave the vessel, there was again a pressing crowd since all wanted to get off the freighter first. Naturally, the Nazis were the first to leave the ship. It appeared that rank, even in the last hours of the deplorable war, still had its privileges. Of course, in our humble opinion, the Third Reich and all its brown splendor had almost fallen apart and was breathing its last, but the Nazis kept up the charade until the very end. Why is it so hard to let go of pride?

I figured they should learn the lesson from the little brook I observed in the woods near Stolp with its Brown trout. The big trout always eat the little trout—and that was exactly what the allied forces did to the Third Reich. Regrettably, in that process the world suffered with them.

Chapter 7

Before the army trucks took the refugees away, all men, regardless of age, were asked to step aside and were enlisted in the Volkssturm. Yes, the Nazis were true to their motto that they would fight to the last man. In their devotion to follow Hitler, they did not heed Scripture, which warns explicitly of the consequences when one follows after a blind leader (Luke 6:39). Among those men enlisted was Dad's one brother-in-law, Uncle Otto Schulz. He was somewhat older than Dad. He had come on one of the other freighters. Dad tried to talk him into remaining with us, but to no avail. He had to go along. Shortly before the collapse of the Third Reich, he was killed in Schleswig Holstein. His family, who did not get away when Stolp was evacuated, were killed by the Russian army when they came through town.

While the Volkssturm recruits were loaded onto a different ship, the army trucks took all other refugees to an evacuated school in Frederiksberg. Here we were assigned to a large classroom on the third floor with five other families. Each of the four corners of the room were occupied by a family, with the last family occupying the center of the room. Our family was able to claim one of the corners right by a window. We put our bedrolls on the floor. After some time we were given straw to make our hard "beds" a little more comfortable. At first there were about 350 refugees in the school, but in only a few days that number grew to a thousand.

Most of the families who shared the classroom with us came from East and West Prussia. And all had gruesome stories to tell about their escape from the advancing Russian armies. The atrocities that were committed on both sides in those war days on the innocent civilian population are still crying to heaven like the blood of innocent Abel, whom his brother Cain slew out of mere jealousy. As we shared, we heard about how some refugees tried to escape in wagons across the frozen sea. However, the warplanes bombed the ice so that the wagons, with their horses and people and goods fell into the icy water and perished.

As we settled into our new surroundings, we knew we needed to find food. Our meager supply had dwindled to a few pieces of dried bread and a rind of stale old cheese. This seemed like a hopeless situation, but once again we turned to our heavenly Father and asked Him to guide us and provide for us. We then set to work seeing what doors the Lord would open. We were like the little sparrows in that Pomeranian farmyard I mentioned in the introduction of my story—we went in search of food. Dad had learned from the camp nurse who had treated his wounded arm that only a block or two away was a navy hospital. After three long days and still no food, my older sisters determined that it was time to pay the navy hospital a visit. Early the next morning they went to the school gate. To their surprise, they found an old man guarding it who told them that they could not leave the camp. Unbeknown to them, the Nazis had enlisted men to guard the gates so that the refugees would not go and beg for food from the Danish people. However, this was no impediment to my older sisters.

Since they couldn't leave through the front gate, they decided to try the back. It too was locked, but it was not nearly as guarded as the front gate. When the guard at the back went around the corner toward the front gate, they jumped the fence and disappeared in the opposite direction and headed for the navy hospital. When they got to the sentry box, one of the two guards told them that he could not permit them to enter the hospital. However, Irmgard didn't take no for an answer and told him she would enter in anyway. When they saw how determined my sisters were, one sentry told the other that he would take them to the guard office. Once in front of his superior, the sentry informed the officer on duty that my sisters had come from the refugee camp in the school building because they had not had anything to eat for the last three days.

The officer looked at them with pity and told them that it was not the navy's duty to supply the refugee camps with food, but that it was the obligation of the Nazis to procure food for the refugees. Having said that, he promised them that he would try his best to get the matter resolved. He assured them that if the Nazis could or would not feed them then the navy would see to it that the refugees were fed. Then he hollered for the orderly and told him to go through all the rooms and collect all the food that he possibly could find and give it to my sisters. When the sailor finally returned, he had three large paper bags full of food.

When my sisters arrived at the school gate, the same old guard was there. When he saw their bags of food, he was speechless. As soon as Lieschen and Irmgard entered the room, they gave the bags of food to Mother, who immediately began to cry. She was overwhelmed by her emotions and God's never-ending love. She sorted through the food items and first gave some to Mrs. Glaser's three children who lay beside us, as well as to the four small children of a lady from Danzig who was across from us. Then she fed Renate and me. After that she gave food to all the adults in the room, including Dad and my older sisters. Last of all she took some for herself. After all had been divided among the families in our room, there was only some bread left over.

Late the next day, around 11:00 p.m., the Nazis brought some hot soup and dry bread to the camp. This good news spread like fire through the whole school, and soon everyone was in a better mood. The kind navy officer had kept his promise. However, most families faced the same dilemma that we found ourselves in; namely, we didn't have enough eating utensils. We all lacked plates or spoons, but in the end we all got fed somehow. After a few days we were supplied with old metal eating utensils, which solved the problem. Thinking back to those first few weeks in the refugee camp and the food we received, I still can't believe we survived, for most of the time that soup looked like pig slop. But since beggars can't be choosers and supposedly "hunger is always the best cook," as my dad so aptly put it, we had no other choice but to eat that "slop," which is how we all survived.

Shortly after we arrived at the school, typhoid fever and dysentery broke out among the badly starved and lice infested refugees. Two of the four children of the lady from Danzig died in our room. My sister Renate as well as my dear mother were sick with dysentery for six long weeks. The only medicine that was dispensed were charcoal tablets. Ironically, quite a number of refugees who had survived all kinds of adverse situations while fleeing the war died in the relative safety of the camp.

In the midst of our grim situation, there were some fun and humorous moments. As everyone knows, children make friends rather easily, and young boys are no exception. So it was only a matter of days before I had found some friends. A few of them I had gotten to know on the freighter as we crossed the Baltic Sea. Most boys love to explore, and we were no exception. But where do you wander and explore in the confines of a rather small and restricted school yard? Since we did not have to go to school, we had lots of spare time on our hands, and after our group had thoroughly explored our immediate surroundings, we felt it was time to venture out into the unknown beyond the school yard. Of course, this was strictly prohibited, but our young and restless spirits disregarded those restrictions in our quest to explore the unknown places beyond the fence.

First and foremost, we had to avoid the guards. Once we figured that out, we jumped the fence and set off to explore the strange new world of wonderful Copenhagen. Fortunately, although we had a sense of adventure, we had a healthy sense of fear of being caught by the guards and not knowing the language. Naturally, we didn't know a single word of Danish! But boy did we learn fast! However, before we learned a single word, we figured out how to beg for money and how to avoid the authorities. You could spot a refugee in the crowd on the sidewalk a mile away because we all "looked alike" with our unkempt and dirty clothes, the trademarks of a refugee! I am not in the least trying to make fun or degrade people in this deplorable situation, after all, I was a refugee for three and a half years and know quite well what stigma is attached to their life! But that was the truth. And yes, as every honest soul knows, the truth can hurt.

The German military police that we now and then encountered on the streets generally had other things on their minds than catching refugee kids on the loose. Sometimes, however, when we caused a bit too much disturbance on the streets, they would take us by the neck and drag us back to camp or they would dispense "street justice," a good licking, that is, which most likely was well deserved. Anyway, after we had begged enough money, mostly of convalescent German soldiers whom we met on our excursions, but also from kind-looking Danish folk, we visited the nearest *Konditorei* (pastry shop). And once the most important task was done, namely to decide which of the many mouthwatering pastries to pick, we would point with our fingers to indicate to the baker which ones we wanted to buy and place our money on the counter. Since we didn't know the currency of the area, the baker took whatever was his and gave us back the rest. Sometimes we did not have enough cash, so we would head back to the street to panhandle a bit longer to get the needed *kronors*.

Sometimes the baker or the people in the store would have enough of us and throw us out the door. But we didn't let that offend or discourage us. We would just look for a friendlier baker. We were a tenacious little bunch. Occasionally, however, we ran into real trouble in the form of a Danish gang of boys who were out to bash refugee kids. We understood that not everyone liked us, after all, we belonged to the hated invaders, even though we poor refugees would have liked nothing more than to have stayed at home where we were born. But such are the fortunes, or perhaps more correctly the misfortunes, of dirty politics.

The street fights usually started with words like, *"De tyske svin hund"* (You German pig dogs!) After we learned what they were saying, we just turned the words around and shouted: *"De danske svin hund!"* How I wish we would have learned to run away from trouble, but when one is young and stupid, one doesn't remember the admonitions of his mother from that very morning. This shouting match went on for some time until the heated insults turned to stones. If nobody broke up the fight, the fists came out and then the real fight was on. And since we were usually outnumbered, we often pulled the shorter end of the stick. At that point, we would quickly retreat into the safer confines of our camp where the adversaries were not permitted.

Fortunately, the gangs did not represent the Danish people as a whole. After I got to know some of the Danish people in the privacy of their homes, I learned to love them, and I will always appreciate their pity and the kindness they showed to us as poor refugees, letting us stay in their nice country after the cessation of hostilities and caring for us those many years we sojourned there until we were permitted to return to Germany. (In our case we were allowed to return in 1948.) When I think how they as a nation had to suffer under the oftentimes heavy-handed German invaders, I could easily understand that they hated all Germans for decades to come. Thank God that time heals wounds!

With the German capitulation on May 8, 1945, a struggle for supremacy arose between different political factions in Denmark. Even though we, as refugees, were innocent bystanders, now and then we suffered the consequences of that struggle, especially from the communist factions. Many a night they came into our camp and, in their search for hiding German soldiers, tore us from our sleep. We then were told to stand in line in the hallway while they searched for the soldiers and also money. One night after they did not find any soldiers, they started to molest a tall, seventeen-year-old lad from West Prussia, whom they accused of having been in the German army. After treating him very roughly, they wanted to drag him away, perhaps to shoot him. Only after much hollering and lamenting by his crying mother did they finally let go of him.

Once these guerilla fighters were drunk, they were incalculable. Some nights we had rifle fire around the school building when two factions got into an argument over who controlled the local piece of turf. And once some of these fighters even bombarded the school's caretaker's house with a mortar launcher. Luckily, no one was home at the time.

Thankfully, the Danish military got the upper hand in these struggles and began to protect the refugee camps. One day after the Danish military had taken over, and much to our surprise I might add, some officers appeared and demanded all our money. They also wanted to inspect the men's identity papers. Since Dad had all his papers handy, particularly those that certified that he had been unfit for military service, he had no problem clarifying his status. Upon reading his paperwork, the tone in their voice grew noticeably warmer. But they still wanted our money. Naturally, you had to be as wise as serpents and as harmless as doves, just as Jesus suggested in the book of Matthew.

While my parents had some money handy for the case of an inspection, most had been sewed in bundles in cloth belts. When we got wind of an inspection, Irmgard would hide these bundles on the outside wall of the school building. The wall was covered with creeping vine tendrils that concealed the money belts. Dad admonished her to make sure the bundles were tucked in securely so that they would not fall down in case it stormed. When the inspection was over, she would retrieve the money.

Right after the Danish military took over, much to our dismay, all our escapades over the fence and into the outside world came abruptly to an end. No more visits to the pastry shop or anywhere else for that matter. From then on we were kept like sheep in a fold, with armed soldiers watching our every move.

While the wound in Dad's arm got better with time, his rheumatism flared up again and got so bad that he was admitted to a hospital. Dad stayed in the hospital for several weeks. The doctors who treated him assured him that they were doing their best, however, in order to cure him, they needed an injection that they did not have at their disposal. But what they did seemed to help him.

When we visited Dad in the hospital, provided we had Danish money, we would visit one of the pastry shops and buy some goodies to share with the kids in our room. Because we had a written permit from the Danish camp officials to visit the hospital, our side trip to the pastry shop was legal!

Chapter 8

As we fled for our lives, we lost every earthly possession we owned except for the clothes on our back and a few other little things. Among those things was our family Bible. And let me tell you, that Bible became even more special to us as we ran for our lives and lived through such difficult days. In the refugee camp, with practically nothing to do, everybody had lots of time on their hands. So the few Bibles in the camp were used a lot.

When times are tough—and they still were tough for us refugees, all had lost house and home and nobody knew what the future had in store for any of us—people are more inclined than at any other time in their life to study or at least read the Word of God. One of those people was my own beloved mother. The adverse situations we had been exposed to on our flight and particularly the miraculous escapes we had experienced stirred my mother's heart. The Lord in His mercy had plucked us out the fire like the proverbial brand from the burning the Bible talks about.

Now that she had lots of time, she read the passages about the Sabbath that had always troubled her. Together with Dad, they talked about the things that were hard for her to understand. When you come from an evangelical background as she had, there were many things that she could not go along with at first. Everyone who had gone out from the Protestant faith was a heretic to her, and she believed that Seventh-day Adventists were a sect. But the more she read and the more she discussed things with Dad, it seemed the more she wanted to know about the whole matter. She was searching for the truth, and the Holy Spirit was certainly leading her.

Dad had never forced the matter of religion on Mom when we lived in Stolp, and he didn't force it now. He let her study for herself and gave her time to digest the new truths she was learning. God is love and does not force anyone to believe in Him or His precious word. He wants people to respond to His love, which He abundantly pours out on all His creatures. Only service that comes as a response to this love is acceptable in His sight. Force, particularly in religious matters, is only used by the adversary of souls. God can and will not force a decision in spiritual things. He created us as free moral beings who have the power of choice. But if we decide we want to follow Him as a response to His never ending love, He will be very, very happy. Jesus said that heaven rejoices when a sinner repents (Luke 15:7).

In addition to helping Mom understand various Bible truths, Dad shared the good news with other refugees. Many people with whom he discussed the Ten Commandments did not believe that there was any merit in keeping them. Most thought that the fourth commandment only belonged to the Jews. Christians kept Sunday. They argued that if there was anything wrong with keeping Sunday, Martin Luther would have known about it and shared that piece of truth. When Dad shared with them how the seventh-day Sabbath had slowly been changed from the day that God had created, to the day that the Red Beast, as he called it, had arbitrarily invented, a few of his listeners actually believed him. But as a result of all these discussions about Sabbath, Dad was soon known as the guy who believed in the Jewish Sabbath.

One day soon after Germany's capitulation, some guy came looking for Dad, and we wondered if he was in some kind of trouble. But then he told us that there was a young couple at the school gate asking if there were any Seventh-day Adventists among the refugees. The people by the gate who heard the question did not know what this young couple was talking about, but when the young man asked if there was someone in the camp who kept the Sabbath, one fellow who had heard Dad talk about the seventh-day Sabbath went over to them and said that he knew someone who always talked about the Sabbath. The young man requested that they fetch Dad. And that was the guy who came looking for Dad.

Dad naturally accompanied the man to the gate, and to his utter surprise, the young man by the gate turned out to be a Seventh-day Adventist preacher by the name of Egon Skold Nielsen. He had come to invite us and any other believers that might be in the camp to join his congregation on Sabbath. Dad thanked them heartily for the invitation and told the couple that he would go and get his family so that they could meet us. In a few minutes, Dad had gathered us together, and soon we were at the school gate meeting the Nielsens. And what a meeting it was! We had never seen these kind folk before, and yet we all had the rather strange feeling as if we knew them from long ago. This impression, I believe, was because of the loving kindness that emanated from the couple.

Here were true Christians who loved their Lord so much that they could not help but love their enemies as well. You must understand, dear friend, that loving your enemy in the midst of a war could turn your own countrymen against you. The stakes were high. But nothing deterred the Nielsens and other Christians like them from obeying their Lord's request to love their enemies (Luke 6:27, 35). Before they said goodbye, they assured us that they would be at the gate on Sabbath morning to pick us up.

When they left, Mom's eyes filled with tears. How could we go to church with them in our filthy clothes? At once Mom and my older sisters got busy washing clothes. Although they didn't have any soap, they did the best they could. Since nobody had an iron to press the clothes after they dried, they were very wrinkly. But we figured that at least some of the dirt had been removed. As I mentioned before, we had our own little animal farms in the form of all the pesky vermin such as lice, fleas, and bedbugs. This, I'm sure, did not go unnoticed by the Danish authorities, and one nice day we were ordered to be deloused. We decided that at least we wouldn't take these little critters to church to infest some unsuspecting churchgoer.

The delousing process involved washing your hair with a liquid called Sabadil vinegar. If a person had lots of hair lice and had scratched the scalp to the point of bleeding, this vinegar mixture burned like fire in the open sores. After our hair dried, we had to comb it with special combs that caught the eggs that had been deposited on the hair. Many of the girls with long hair cried during this process since the comb pulled their hair and hurt considerably. After one was done with the hair, you had to go and stand in another line, males separate from females, for the rest of the delousing procedure. Everybody had to open their shirts and then the nurse dusted you with a liberal amount of a stinking powder that was supposed to take care of the lice on your body and clothes. Then the nurse asked you to open your pants so that she could put some more of that stinking stuff down your waist. Soon the whole place stunk like the powder, and the air was full of dust, which resulted in everyone coughing and sputtering.

Just when we thought we were done, we were told to stand in yet another line to get some shots to protect us against diseases. My friend Erich had been brave thus far, but when he saw the doctor with the large syringe and heard some other kids crying, he flipped out. He threw himself on the floor and screamed and kicked. His mom couldn't calm him down, so two men finally grabbed him and tried to hold him so that the doctor could give him the injection in his upper arm. But Erich grew wilder. He pulled and jerked until the doctor had had enough. He told the men to put Erich on his lap and his mom to pull down his pants, and then he jammed the needle into Erich's buttock. When Erich felt the needle, he screamed like a pig when it knows it's going to be slaughtered. Erich then jammed his teeth into the doctor's thigh. That's what one might call a chain reaction, I suppose. However, the chain reaction was not done yet, since the last "link" of that chain followed right after the bite in the form of two lickings, one from the doctor and one from his mom. Times were different back then, and in addition to parents, persons in authority had the right to physically discipline children who they felt were misbehaving.

When I saw what had happened to Erich, I started to shake like an aspen leaf in the wind. However, when it was my turn to be inoculated by the good doctor, the kind nurse talked softly to me, and I didn't cry until after he had administered the shot. That was quite an ordeal for us kids.

Finally, Sabbath morning arrived, and we dressed and waited by the gate for the Nielsens. When they arrived to pick us up, they told us that they had obtained permission for us to be with them all day. They mentioned that they had to guarantee that we would not run away or cause any other trouble. Even though they did not know us, they had pledged to the camp officials that we would return in the evening. Such was their trust in us as fellow brothers and sisters in Christ.

On the other side of the gate, we boarded a streetcar that took us a few blocks from the church. We then walked the rest of the way. Some of the Danes stared at us, but we tried not to notice. When we arrived at the church, an elderly women came straight to us and introduced herself as Sister Schmied. She told us she would interpret for us, and she then invited us to come to her place for dinner. Again, I am compelled to thank these kindhearted folks for all they did for us and many other refugees, for, as we soon found out, we were not the only refugees they had invited to their church service. I will never forget the friendship these people demonstrated to their country's enemies. Their kindness and love helped me take my stand for Christ.

I honestly don't remember what Pastor Nielsen said in his sermon that morning, but I do remember the delicious meal we had at Sister Schmied's home afterwards. Besides us, she invited another refugee family, and together we thanked God for His many blessings. After dinner the Nielsens came over, and soon the adults were relating to our Danish friends how marvelously God had cared for us during the war. (Many years later at a camp meeting in Canada, I met a brother from Denmark to whom I shared our experience in Copenhagen. After listening to my story, he told me that Sister Schmied was his mother! Praise God for his family!)

All too soon it was time to leave, but before we left, we enjoyed some mouthwatering Danish sandwiches. When the Nielsens dropped us off at the camp, they told us that from now on we would be picked up every Sabbath morning for church by a church member or them. This arrangement continued for about a year until we were moved from Copenhagen to Rom per Lemvig in Jutland, close to Lemsfjord.

Over time life improved somewhat in the refugee camp. However, we were still not allowed to go beyond the confines of the fence that surrounded the school property, which was frustrating. Fortunately, our family at least got to see something of the outside world every Sabbath when we went to church. Regrettably few other refugees enjoyed such a privilege.

Summer came and went and life passed by rather uneventfully. People say that no news is good news, but that only goes so far, and then one wants to know what life has in store for the future. To those of us in the refugee camp, it seemed that the outside world had completely forgotten us. There was no news as to what would happen to us or when we could go home. It was hard waiting on the government to make up their mind as to what to do with us. Many older people were heartbroken and homesick. But most held out hope that we would be allowed to return to Germany someday soon.

While the people in the camp pondered their uncertain future, Dad tried to sow seeds of hope in the sure Word of God with those who would listen. He told them that the good news of the Bible was the only hope for an ailing society and a dying world. He enjoyed good discussions about the Word of God with some, while others shrugged it off and told him boldly that if there was a God in heaven, He should have prevented the horrible war and all its atrocities. When Dad explained to them that God had created man as a free moral agent and had given him the power of choice, they seemed perplexed. He told them that God hates war, but He allows people to do as they wish, and our political leaders chose to go to war. Some of the men who had been listening to Dad got angry with him when he mentioned that the Nazis were to blame for the suffering, while others agreed with him.

They wanted to blame God for the misery they were experiencing, when they should have blamed Satan. Only when Satan, the instigator of all human suffering, is destroyed will this earth and its inhabitants see everlasting peace. Until such a time, we have to suffer the consequences of sin whether we like it or not.

Fall arrived with brilliant colors and for the most part lots of sunshine. The leaves of the wild vine growing on the walls of the school building turned crimson red and the few trees in the school yard a golden yellow. All nature seemed aglow, while the empty hearts of the refugees seemed dim. Yes, we had been saved by God's grace, but our future seemed bleak in the camp. Not even all the beauty of fall was able to transform that gloom and sadness into joy.

And then a season of foggy weather arrived that seemed to turn the gloom into bottomless doom. People became quite agitated with each other, and instead of turning to God in their misery, they turned on each other. With too much time on our hands and nothing to do, all the while living in cramped quarters together, people started growing more and more restless.

For example, our little gang of refugee boys had been watching some fruit tress that grew across the school's perimeter fence all summer long. Now in fall the apples and pears that graced the fruit-laden branches seemed to radiate with an almost mesmerizing attractive power. In particular, one apple tree stands out in my memory as holding the biggest apples I had ever seen. Those large apples were simply irresistible! With their shining red surface, they seemed to beckon to us from across the fence.

I am not proud of what I did one early morning, and I did not boast about my bad deed in front of the other boys in our gang. In fact, I did not say a single word to anyone, not even my parents or sisters. In the concealing fog one morning, I quietly climbed the seven-foot high chain-link fence. My young heart pounded wildly from excitement and fear of getting caught. When I reached the top, I carefully climbed over the strands of barbwire and scurried down the other side of the fence. Once on the ground, I looked around to see if I had been detected. All was quiet. The only noise I heard came from the heavy water drops that fell from the leaves. I rushed over to the wooden garden fence and jumped over. Even though it was quite foggy, I had no problem finding the right tree—the one with the large apples. To my utter surprise, most of them had disappeared. I took the two that had been forgotten and put them in my pants pockets. This was easier said than done since the apples were so huge. After a little struggle, I had them securely hidden inside my pockets and I tried to jump over the garden fence. However, with the big apples in my pockets, I couldn't move as easily as before.

Suddenly I heard irate Danish voices coming from the house. In seconds sweet victory abruptly turned into a headless, confused retreat. I made it over the garden fence and rushed to the perimeter fence. I started to climb it, but those bulging apples were in the way. Besides that, my bare feet were wet, and they kept slipping as I tried to climb the chain-link fence. But what was worse was the battle that raged in my mind. *Why did you steal those apples?* I heard a voice say clearly. *You know you should not steal!* I instantly remembered the words of the eighth commandment: Thou shalt not steal! The voice continued, *You are such a bad boy! God will never forgive you for this.* I looked around, but I was alone.

My breath came in short gasps and my heart pounded like never before. When I got to the barbwire, I heard someone running through the garden. The thought that I would soon be caught flashed through my mind and gave me the boost to get over the barbwire. But when I jumped down to the school yard, one pant leg got caught on the barbwire and tore a hole in the garment and my leg. To make matters worse, when I landed on the pavement, I sprained both of my ankles, which was very painful. As I lay there on the ground, I saw a very angry looking man on the other side of the fence. He hurled all kinds of Danish curses at me.

I clenched my teeth to deal with the pain and staggered toward the big doors of the school. Once inside, I contemplated my next move. I did not dare go up to our room and face my parents. Instead I limped down a flight of stairs to the basement and hid in one of the washrooms. I waited there for a long time—every minute I expected to hear a guard come in the washroom searching for me. The battle inside continued. By now my conscience was tormenting me almost beyond what I could bear. And in my distress I promised God that I would never disappoint Him again or steal another apple. I promised to be a good boy for the rest of my life. I promised God many other things that morning, most of which I do not remember anymore. And since all these promises were born out of fear of being punished by a vengeful, angry God, they regrettably remained only empty promises.

Many years later when I had grown in my spiritual life, I contemplated this situation and determined that Lucifer works like this. First, he tempts a person into breaking God's law. Then he accuses and mentally torments the sinner into thinking that he is lost. But I also learned that in Christ our Savior, we have an advocate who understands our weaknesses and who pleads on our behalf. Listen to what Ellen G. White, a person with great insight in spiritual things, has to say about this very subject: "While Jesus is pleading for the subjects of His grace, Satan accuses them before God as transgressors. The great deceiver has sought to lead them into skepticism, to cause them to lose confidence in God, to separate themselves from His love, and to break His law. Now he points to the record of their lives, to the defects of character, the unlikeness to Christ, which has dishonored their Redeemer, to all the sins that he has tempted them to commit, and because of these he claims them as his subjects" (*The Great Controversy*, p. 484).

God knew that a sinner, converted or not, could never on his own obey the law. Sin has weakened our moral powers to the point where we have lost all ability to withstand our evil, natural tendencies and our wily foe. And since God loves sinners, He sent His Son to do for sinners what they are unable to do for themselves, namely redeem themselves from sin. John sums up God's great love for sinners in the well-known text, John 3:16: "For God so loved the world, that he gave his only begotten Son, that whosoever believeth in him should not perish, but have everlasting life." Therefore, we do not have to despair when we fall to temptations. If we repent, Jesus will pardon our sins. But we have to believe in Him and His atoning blood.

Time moved slowly by and soon December arrived, bringing with it much colder weather. Unfortunately, most of us had very poor footwear. During the war it had been very hard to get leather shoes, and the substitute leather shoes that most of us were wearing had big holes in them. With winter knocking on the door, we worried about our feet staying warm. Then one day someone got the idea that we could use the straw from our beds to fabricate a type of footwear. This was before the invention of the combine, so the straw was not chopped up and was long enough to braid. To make a "shoe sole," one braided a long strand of straw rope and then bent the end of the rope over some inches and stitched the bent over piece to the rope. Once this was started, all you had to do was continue the process until you had an oblong or elliptical piece of sewn together straw that was big enough for your foot and shaped like a sole.

We then tailored the top part of the shoe from some old piece of material, perhaps a soldiers' uniform found lying around in some hidden corner. The upper part of the shoe was then sewn to the straw sole. Creativity resulted in a brand new pair of winter footwear! The only trouble with the shoes was that they didn't last too long because of the fragile nature of the straw and the thread with which the sole was stitched together. The production of straw footwear was, therefore, an ongoing job.

Then one day Pastor Nielsen and his charming wife, together with other church members, arrived at the camp with lots of cardboard boxes. They asked the astonished camp officials if they were permitted to distribute what the church had collected for the children of our camp. Word quickly spread that all the children should assemble at the camp office. We wondered what was in store for us. Since it wasn't Christmas yet, we did not expect any gifts, but boy were we in for a surprise. All the children of the entire camp received a pair of shoes! Some were new, others used, but all of us were very happy and thankful for the unselfish and kindhearted Danish people for their generosity! This was another example of these good folks following Christ's command to love their enemies. It is hard to conquer selfishness and pride under normal circumstances, but particularly in the aftermath of a war, where the natural tendency is to hate your enemy, these people demonstrated the power of God's love! They were truly disciples of Christ, for "by this shall all men know that ye are my disciples, if ye have love one to another" (John 13:35).

The Danish Adventists had yet another surprise for us. But before I tell you what it was, I first must tell about the story of our *Tannenbaum* (Christmas tree). Christmas was just around the corner and there was no Christmas tree in sight. While this might have been bearable for the adults, it was a major catastrophe for all the children in the camp. It was lucky that there wasn't one growing on the school's property or, in all likelihood, it would have been chopped down and ended up in the school's auditorium for the Nativity play.

There were many handy men in the camp among the refugees, but one middle-aged fellow surpassed them all. In wise foresight, he had started weeks before Christmas to carve us a tree. He had found scraps of old lumber somewhere from which he had laboriously whittled a little masterpiece. With his skilled and patient hands and aided by a razor-sharp pocketknife, he first made the stem. Then he whittled the larger branches, drilled holes into the stem at certain intervals, and glued the branches in. After he had carved the smaller branches, he glued them to the larger branches, and our improvised

Tannenbaum was almost ready. To imitate the needles on the branches, he had carefully used his sharp knife to curl thin shavings on the small branches. After all had been glued together, he painted the whole tree green with some water color that he had scrounged someplace. The four- or five-foot creation certainly had the semblance of an evergreen "tree."

Once the tree was done, some of the man's friends made little stars and birds and all kinds of other things to hang on the branches. But we still needed tinsel. Some very creative people asked the smokers among the refugees for the tinsel paper with which the cigarette packages were lined, and this became the tinsel for our Christmas tree. However, one final thing was missing—candles for the tree. These could not be made like all the other things, and so, sadly, the little masterpiece of creativity and skill was not complete according to German tradition.

On Christmas Eve we gathered in the auditorium to watch the Nativity play. There on the platform stood the artificial Christmas tree in all its "splendor." It seemed a little dull without candles; however, this was overshadowed by the shining faces of the children singing with fervor. Quite soon after the play was over and we had gone back to our rooms, much to all the children's surprise, Santa Claus arrived in the form of Pastor Nielsen and his helpers. They went from classroom to classroom and gave a present to each and every child in our camp. Oh what excitement when I opened my present. Underneath the wrapping I found a box with a log cabin printed on its lid. I marveled at the picture of the log cabin and opened the box. There was an instruction sheet in Danish on how to assemble the little cabin, which didn't help me since I didn't know the language. But that didn't stop me. In no time I had that log cabin assembled, and I immediately fell in love with it. Ever since that time I have had an interest in log structures.

That night when I was told to go to bed, I disassembled my little cabin, put it back into its box, and slept with it securely tucked in my arms. People were very thankful for those wonderful Christians who did so much, especially for the children in our refugee camp.

My parents, Paul and Martha Stüwe, and sister Renate.

Chapter 9

In March of 1946 we were moved to a refugee camp in Rom per Lemvig. We stayed there for about a year before we were moved again, this time to a camp close to Oxbol in southwestern Denmark. The Oxbol camp was rather large, housing approximately 45,000 refugees. Shortly after being moved to Oxbol, Dad and Lieschen were permitted to return to Germany. Lieschen had found out through the Red Cross that her husband was living in Köln/Cologne, and she was allowed to join him. And since men were needed to rebuild Germany, Dad could go too. We were informed that the rest of our family had to stay behind and wait until things had normalized in Germany before we could return.

Mother continued to study her Bible and so did Irmgard. Somehow my sister found out that there were some families meeting together for Friday vespers in one of the school barracks. One of the families by the name of Schitteck had several children my age, and we soon became close friends. Those vespers in Oxbol left a lasting impression on me. At one meeting I learned one of my favorite hymns, "O Hast Thou Ne'er Heard of the Beautiful Stream," by poet Richard Torrey. After singing a few hymns, one of the ladies would teach us kids Bible stories by way of a picture scroll. How I loved to hear the story of David the shepherd boy and mighty Goliath.

The day finally came when we were sent back to Germany. Since Stalin had been allowed by the Allied Commanders to drive all German people out of the eastern provinces of East Prussia, West Prussia, Pomerania, and also part of Silesia, we could not return home. Stolp had become, by Allied consent and permission, part of Poland. And my parents did not want to move to East Germany, also known as the German Democratic Republic, for the communists were ruling the roost there. And frankly, we had had enough from the brown dictator and his henchmen who destroyed our country and brought hate and misery to millions of people. Under no circumstances would Dad allow us to move to the realm of the red dictators. On the other hand, he did not want us to move to where he lived either. The totally destroyed Ruhr valley was no place for a family. But where should we go? Fortunately, God had the answer!

Irmgard had worked as a letter carrier in the Oxbol refugee camp, which allowed her to become acquainted with a woman who promised to help us when she moved back to southern Germany. The Allied forces had divided Germany into four zones. The Russian zone later became the German Democratic Republic and the American, English and French zones joined together to form the Federal Republic of Germany. The location where the young women lived belonged to the French zone. For unknown reasons, the French allowed only relatively small numbers of refugees to be admitted to their zone even though that part of Germany was not as badly destroyed as other areas.

However, as she had promised, the young woman went to the authorities where she lived and requested a permit for us to move there. It took some time for the papers to be processed, but in the end we were permitted to move to the French zone, ending up in the little town of Ebingen in the Swabian Alb region. Although it felt good to be back in Germany, we were faced with a new challenge. The people of the Swabian Alb region spoke a dialect that was very different from the high German we were used to. I found it hard to understand that we were back in Germany when I couldn't understand the German people in my new community. Our only saving grace was that all Germans had to learn the so-called high German language in school, so our new neighbors at least understood us. We just had a hard time understanding them.

Soon after we arrived in the little town, my mother and Irmgard asked if there was a congregation of Seventh-day Adventists in town. To their regret, not many people knew about this denomination, or sect, as they called it. They suggested we join one of the real churches in the town. Mother gently declined.

As we got to know our neighbors, we shared with them our miraculous escape during the war. What I found interesting was how people reacted. The more educated, well-to-do individuals would tell me that it was simply fate that we had survived those situations and that it hadn't been our time yet. Only a few agreed that perhaps a merciful God had something to do with these experiences. But more often than not, the question was asked, "Why did God permit all that pain and suffering? Why, if there is a God at all, did He allow the war to continue? Or at least, why didn't He help to win the war and end it sooner?"

While I readily admit that I don't have the answers to all the "whys," deep down in my heart I believe and am fully persuaded that a merciful God did not want that horrible bloodshed and destruction; neither was He responsible for it. Those who blame God for the war simply do not know Him. God is love, and out of His love He created human beings with the power of choice! It was a risk God was willing to take. When Adam and Eve chose to disobey, sin entered the world with all of its consequences. God did not prevent Eve and Adam from making the wrong choice. He could not do so. Had He done so, He would have taken their freedom of choice away and become a dictator like Hitler. We humans must realize that we are responsible for our choices and must suffer the consequences of our choices without blaming someone else for them.

There are so many who blame God for all the bad things that go on in this world when the blame should really be laid at the feet of Satan. When the farmers' crops are destroyed by hail or when tornados and twisters destroy villages and the like, God is blamed for it. The media often declares it as an act of God, but we know from the book of Job that Satan is behind it all:

> Now there was a day when the sons of God came to present themselves before the Lord, and Satan came also among them. And the Lord said unto Satan, Whence comest thou?
> Then Satan answered the Lord, and said, From going to and fro in the earth, and from walking up and down in it.
> And the Lord said unto Satan, Hast thou considered my servant Job, that there is none like him in the earth, a perfect and an upright man, one that feareth God, and escheweth evil?
> Then Satan answered the Lord, and said, Doth Job fear God for nought? Hast not thou made an hedge about him, and about his house, and about all that he hath on every side? thou hast blessed the work of his hands, and his substance is increased in the land. But put forth thine hand now, and touch all that he hath, and he will curse thee to thy face.
> And the Lord said unto Satan, Behold, all that he hath is in thy power; only upon himself put not forth thine hand. So Satan went forth from the presence of the Lord. And there was a day when his sons and his daughters were eating and drinking wine in their eldest brother's house: And there came a messenger unto Job, and said, The oxen were plowing, and the asses feeding beside them: And the Sabeans fell upon them, and took them away; yea, they have slain the servants with the edge of the sword; and I only am escaped alone to tell thee. While he was yet speaking, there came also another, and said, The fire of God is fallen from heaven, and hath burned up the sheep, and the servants, and consumed them; and I only am escaped alone to tell thee. While he was yet speaking, there came also another, and said, The Chaldeans made out three bands, and fell upon the camels, and have carried them away, yea, and slain the servants with the edge of the sword; and I only am escaped alone to tell thee. While he was yet speaking, there came also another, and said, Thy sons and thy daughters were eating and drinking wine in their eldest brother's house: And, behold, there came a great wind from the wilderness, and smote the four corners of the house, and it fell upon the young men, and they are dead; and I only am escaped alone to tell thee.
> Then Job arose, and rent his mantle, and shaved his head, and fell down upon the ground, and worshipped, And said, Naked came I out of my mother's womb, and naked shall I return thither: the Lord gave, and the Lord hath taken away; blessed be the name of the Lord. In all this Job sinned not, nor charged God foolishly. (Job 1:6–22)

In this biblical narrative we read about a meeting between the sons of God and God. Although he was a fallen angel, Satan attended the meeting. When God heard that Satan had been up to his usual tricks, namely walking to and fro on the earth, He asked Satan if he had seen how Job lived his life. At once Satan accused Job of serving God out of mere selfish ambitions because of the blessings God had bestowed upon him. Satan said that Job would curse God to His face if he was tested. And God agreed to the test. He was sure about Job and his devotion to Him. God trusted Job and his genuine love for his Creator.

I think it is important to point out, since this is mostly overlooked, that Job, due to no fault of his own, had to withstand the severest trials and tribulation because of Satan's hatred of God. Satan sought to prove God wrong and tarnish His character. Ever since the beginning of the great conflict between good and evil, Satan has accused God of being a stern and unforgiving dictator whose laws are impossible to keep.

Friends, when we are in a situation like Job, we do well to remember that it is Satan, the adversary, who is responsible for our trials and tribulations and not our loving Father in heaven. We should always remember this important fact when facing trials here on earth.

God permitted Satan to bring about the adversities in Job's life. Satan exhibited diabolical joy as he destroyed Job's earthly possessions, including the lives of his children. The disasters that befell Job reveal that wars, destructive fires and whirlwinds, and all other calamities are not an act of God, but acts of Satan who finds great delight in the destruction that he can cause. Let me point out here that Satan was also created with the power of choice and is, therefore, responsible for the choices he makes, just like you and I!

You would think that after that severe test, in which Job showed his true character by honoring God in the worst of tribulations, Satan would have given in and admitted that God had been right in his assessment of Job. But true to his nature, Satan called for another test that was even more severe than the first one. This too shows you Satan's true character. He is not satisfied unless he has completely destroyed the human being, so that there is no hope of eternal salvation for him. In Job 2:1–10 we read about the next test:

> Again there was a day when the sons of God came to present themselves before the Lord, and Satan came also among them to present himself before the Lord. And the Lord said unto Satan, From whence comest thou? And Satan answered the Lord, and said, From going to and fro in the earth, and from walking up and down in it. And the Lord said unto Satan, Hast thou considered my servant Job, that there is none like him in the earth, a perfect and an upright man, one that feareth God, and escheweth evil? and still he holdeth fast his integrity, although thou movedst me against him, to destroy him without cause. And Satan answered the Lord, and said, Skin for skin, yea, all that a man hath will he give for his life. But put forth thine hand now, and touch his bone and

his flesh, and he will curse thee to thy face. And the LORD said unto Satan, Behold, he is in thine hand; but save his life. So went Satan forth from the presence of the LORD, and smote Job with sore boils from the sole of his foot unto his crown. And he took him a potsherd to scrape himself withal; and he sat down among the ashes. Then said his wife unto him, Dost thou still retain thine integrity? curse God, and die. But he said unto her, Thou speakest as one of the foolish women speaketh. What? shall we receive good at the hand of God, and shall we not receive evil? In all this did not Job sin with his lips.

What can be more trying to our faith than severe sickness and disease that befalls us personally or afflicts our family members? How hard is it for the strongest believers to look beyond the grave that has just swallowed a mother from her young children or taken a father from his growing family? In all such heartrending situations, let us remember that this is not God's design. He wants all of His created beings to live in eternal happiness.

In the case of Job, a person might wonder why God would allow Satan to give Job a second test when he had clearly withstood the first. There is no simple answer to this question. Godlike insight is needed here. But I do believe that God wanted to show Satan beyond a shadow of doubt that Job was not the person Satan accused him to be. And yes, I also believe that this true story has great significance for our lives today—to give us hope when we are suffering severe trials and affliction. When he heard that Job was once more under his power, Satan tormented Job with horrible boils, just as he uses diseases and illnesses to torment people today. I am sure Satan would have taken Job's life, but God did not permit him to do so. Yet even this terrible affliction was not strong enough to destroy Job's faith in God.

At the close of Job's story, we see how Satan tried to make it look as if God was behind all the troubles and suffering in the world. But then we see how a loving God turned Job's affliction completely around and blessed him beyond what he had before (Job 42:12, 13). What a happy ending to an otherwise grim story! And what do we learn from it all? I, for one, have learned that there is no crown without a cross! And by the way, that cross is usually very hard to bear. But when you find yourself stuck above your head in the quagmire of sin and suffering, when all around you seems dark and like there is no way out, and when that cross, in the form of trials and tribulations, almost crushes you, do not give Satan the victory—do not lose your faith in God. Instead, read the story of Job, meditate and pray about it, so that you may receive the insight needed to strengthen your faith. That, I believe, is the main reason why God included the story of Job in His word.

If you still wonder why you have to go through all the trials and tribulations and not your enemies, let me share two statements with you that really opened my eyes. They are from the inspired pen of Ellen G. White. She writes as follows:

> The fact that we are called upon to endure trial proves that the Lord Jesus sees in us something very precious, which he desires to develop. If He saw in us nothing whereby He

might glorify His name He would not spend time in refining us. We do not take special pains in pruning brambles. Christ does not cast worthless stones into His furnace. It is valuable ore that he tests....

The Lord allows His chosen ones to be placed in the furnace of affliction in order that He may see what temper they are of and whether He can mold and fashion them for His work. (*Testimonies for the Church*, vol. 7, p. 214)

It may be that much work needs to be done in your character building, that you are a rough stone, which must be squared and polished before it can fill a place in God's temple. You need not be surprised if with hammer and chisel God cuts away the sharp corners of your character until you are prepared to fill the place He has for you. No human being can accomplish this work. Only by God can it be done. And be assured that He will not strike one useless blow. His every blow is struck in love, for your eternal happiness. He knows your infirmities and works to restore, not to destroy. (Ibid., p. 264)

So here we have the answer to why we experience trials and tribulations. If you ever have hit yourself accidentally with a hammer, you know it hurts. But you also know that it hurts only for a certain time and then the ache and pain disappears. And so it is with our trials and tribulations. After God is through hammering and chiseling, our characters will more closely resemble the character of Christ, which is the most important thing to remember when it hurts! True, this is easier said than done; nevertheless, let us try to remember the end of Job's story and be thankful that our great and merciful heavenly Father has not left us to suffer under Satan's attacks forever. He made a way of escape when He sent His dear Son into our world of sin to die for us, that all who desire to be freed from Satan's power may avail themselves of Christ's salvation.

As we worked to establish a new life for ourselves after the war, we had the opportunity to reflect on these thoughts and share them with others, even if most people struggled with this concept of a loving God and an evil adversary. Although we were on the road to recovery, there were still bumps along the way.

The first few weeks in our new community were spent in a small camp. As soon as the officials found suitable dwellings, they moved the refugee families out of the camp. Never will I forget the first meal we were provided in Ebingen. After we had been settled in the camp some social workers took us to a restaurant, a *Wirtschaft*, as it is called in Swabian. The name of this establishment was *Mohren*. As we later found out, this was quite a popular name for this type of establishment since almost all of the surrounding mountain villages or towns had at least one *Wirtschaft* by that name. The selection of dishes one could order in the restaurant was quite limited at that time. On this particular day the dish being served was *Kuddeln*, a food that was unfamiliar to us. And since a good old Pomeranian saying states, *"Wat de bur nich kennt dat fret hei nich!"* (What the farmer doesn't know, he doesn't eat!), we were in quite a predicament.

On the one hand beggars can't be choosers and these Swabians were giving us the best they could afford. We certainly didn't want to offend them, but the chunks of cow's stomach floating in the soup with the potatoes and carrots and onions made our stomachs turn without even taking a bite! When our family only ate the potatoes and carrots, leaving the ugly-looking chunks of cow's stomach in our deep soup plates, an unpleasant murmuring arose from the guests seated at the tables next to us. They asked if we weren't hungry, for they had grown up eating this dish and thought it was wonderful. We were thankful when we were able to fix our own food the next day. I can assure you that in all the years we lived in the Swabian Alb region, my mother did not prepare *Kuddeln* for us one single time.

There is one more thing I will never forget upon returning to Germany and that was the first candies I tasted after the war. Before we settled in Ebingen, we were moved to a refugee camp on the outskirts of a town named Bieberach. This was almost like paradise, since the camp was practically surrounded by fruit trees. Since it was fall, we ate the ripening fruit—apples, pears, and plums—all day long. Besides that, we were allowed to roam freely around the area. Weather permitting, two other boys and I explored the hilly countryside to our hearts' content. Occasionally, we would accompany my older sister or some of my friends' parents to town. Here we soon found a store that sold candies. However, since we did not have any new German money, we had no means of securing any. And yes, the adults who accompanied us would not let us beg for money. Every time we came to town, we would go and look at the candies in the display window, squeezing our noses flat against the glass.

One beautiful fall day we met an old woman on our cross-country hike who was picking potatoes all by herself. And since we had been raised to be helpful and kind, we politely asked if we could assist her with her chore. She told us that she would greatly appreciate our help. Soon we found out that her son and family were going to come and help. When they arrived, they were surprised to see us there, but were thankful for the extra help. Now the potato digging and picking went really fast. By late afternoon we were done, and the son asked us what he owed us for helping them out. We told them that it had been a pleasure to help them and that they did not owe us anything. But his mother demanded that we should go along with them so that she could give us something for our labor. When we arrived at their home, her son went into the house and came back with fifty pennies in paper money for each of us as well as a huge loaf of home baked bread to divide amongst us. We thanked them for the money and bread and went back to the refugee camp.

Let me assure you that I have never felt that good again when earning money for a job. Those fifty pennies that we received for our labor of love made us think that we were rich. On our way home, those pennies started to burn a hole into our pockets, but since it was too late to visit the candy store, we agreed to do that the next day. It seemed that we could already taste the sweet candies. When I stepped into our room, I ran to my mother and waved the fifty-penny bill in front of her eyes and shouted, "Mom, look! I'm rich! I'm rich!" I was quite proud of myself.

When Mom asked where I had gotten the money from, I told her the story. Then she asked me what I was going to do with the money. I told her that I was going to buy the candies I had seen in the store. She then asked me if I would be willing to give her the money so that we could send a letter to Dad to let him know where we were. As you can imagine, this was a very difficult pill to swallow. But when she told me that Dad would be more than glad to hear how we were doing and where we were, the disappointment slowly disappeared, for I knew that the letter was more important to our family than the candies in the store. So I gave her the money.

That evening Irmgard wrote a long letter to Dad, explaining to him that we were in a camp in Germany but that we might be moved once more. The next day we all went to town to mail the letter. When Irmgard asked the counter clerk at the post office how much the letter would cost to mail, a broad smile spread across her face when she heard the answer. I soon understood the reason for her smile. When she paid for the stamp, the clerk gave her some coins in return, which Irmgard placed into my hand. Now I smiled too. After leaving the post office, we headed over to the candy store and bought some candies with the leftover money. I must say, sharing that money made me feel really good, for I knew I had done the right thing.

One day we were informed by the social workers in Ebingen that they had found a dwelling for us on Christian Landenberger Strasse (street), which was halfway up the Schlossberg mountainside. Having been born in the lowlands of Pomerania, I was very interested in the mountains of the Swabian Alb region. All along the beech-covered slopes, but mainly on the ridges, one could see white rock formations protruding through the forest canopy, which at this time of year was aglow in its beautiful fall colors. I was very content in my new surroundings.

After we moved into our dwelling, Mother went to the public school at the foot of the Schlossberg mountain to enroll me, and with that my freewheeling life came to an abrupt end. As I was busy with school, Irmgard was busy with work. She got a job working in a textile factory, and with the money she earned, she looked after the needs of our family. After I had finished public school, I found a job, and for three years I gave all my earnings to my parents so that our family could survive, since Dad's war invalids' pension income was insufficient for our needs.

While at work one day, Irmgard met and befriended a young war widow. This woman was a local, and when the talk turned to religion one day, she asked my sister to what church she belonged. Irmgard told her that she had gone to the Seventh-day Adventist Church in Stolp, but regrettably she could not find such a church in Ebingen. Her friend told her that she thought there were some Seventh-day Adventists meeting at a certain locality and that she would be happy to show her the place. When Irmgard came home from work that day and told us the news, Mother cried for joy. She was so happy to have found a church because she longed to worship and fellowship with God's people on Sabbath.

When the next Sabbath arrived, the young woman showed my sister where the place was, and Mother, Irmgard, and Renate went to church. I had to go to school and missed out on the excitement of finding the Adventist congregation in Ebingen. However, when I got home from school, Irmgard told me that there was a meeting in the afternoon that we could all attend. We had been unable to find the meeting place of the congregation because it was tucked away in a little side alley.

The afternoon meeting turned out to be quite exciting. Pastor Flammer served three or four small congregations that were scattered over a wide territory, but he was in town, so the church held a special afternoon service that day. For many years Pastor Flammer had been a missionary in Africa and he shared some stories of his life in "the dark continent." The stories he told left a deep impression on me as to his character. I remember one story in particular. He had arrived in a jungle village and was invited to have supper with the chief. Now these good folks gave the best they had to the missionary, a bowl of rice with a fried rat on top as a special treat. The villagers came to watch the missionary eat supper with the chief. If he had declined to eat the food he was offered, he would have destroyed any chances he might have had to spread the gospel there. So he ate of the rice and gave the rat to the chief.

When Pastor Flammer found out that both my mom and Irmgard were interested in the truth, he gave them a series of Bible studies, and at the end of their studies, both wanted to be baptized. We had been in Ebingen a year when Dad was permitted to join us. It was wonderful to be together as a family once again. When he heard of Mom and Irmgard's decision to be baptized, he determined to make a new start in his spiritual life as well. After joining the church and getting acquainted with the members, we soon felt at home in God's family. Time moved forward, and one cold day in January of 1953 I was baptized as well, and some years later Renate also took her stand for Jesus and was baptized.

Satan may have sought to destroy our family during the war, but praise God he did not succeed. We came through with our faith intact. In fact, we all dedicated our lives to following Him, and our love for God grew as we studied His Word.

Do not despair when dark storm clouds loom overhead and you can't see a way out. Turn to Jesus with all your troubles; He is more than willing to help you. Remember too that there is no crown without a cross! That's why Luke wrote: "We must through much tribulation enter into the kingdom of God" (Acts 14:22). And this is what we should be concerned about, entering into the kingdom of God.

I would like to suggest that what we have to watch out for and beware of while we are living on this planet are the good times when we don't have any trials or tribulations. It is during these times that we often slip away from God and become self-reliant. When Satan was unable to destroy the early church by all his cruel inventions, he switched his tactics. Instead of the dungeon, the sword, or the torture chamber with all its cruelties, he introduced good times of peace and relative safety in a world accepting of Christianity. I would like to suggest that, instead of complaining when we face trials and tribulations, we should try to look beyond the hurt and pain and see our difficulties as a means of perfecting our character to be more like Christ.

I do not blame you if you should find this hard to accept, for I do not always see right away God's loving hands in the midst of my trials and pain. But take heart and ask Jesus to open your eyes so that you may see Him during the storm and confidently take hold of His hand in faith. As we fled from the approaching Russian army, we could not see the end from the beginning, but in faith, we clung to the hand of God and the small miracles He performed in the midst of the turmoil and hostilities of the war. Satan sought to destroy us, but God protected us as He did Job, and although we lost everything, God spared our lives. And in the end, we were led to seek a closer walk with the One who gave His precious life for us. It is my prayer that we will all abide in Him until all the trials and tribulations here on earth have come to an end and we can be together with our Lord and Savior Jesus Christ for eternity in His kingdom.

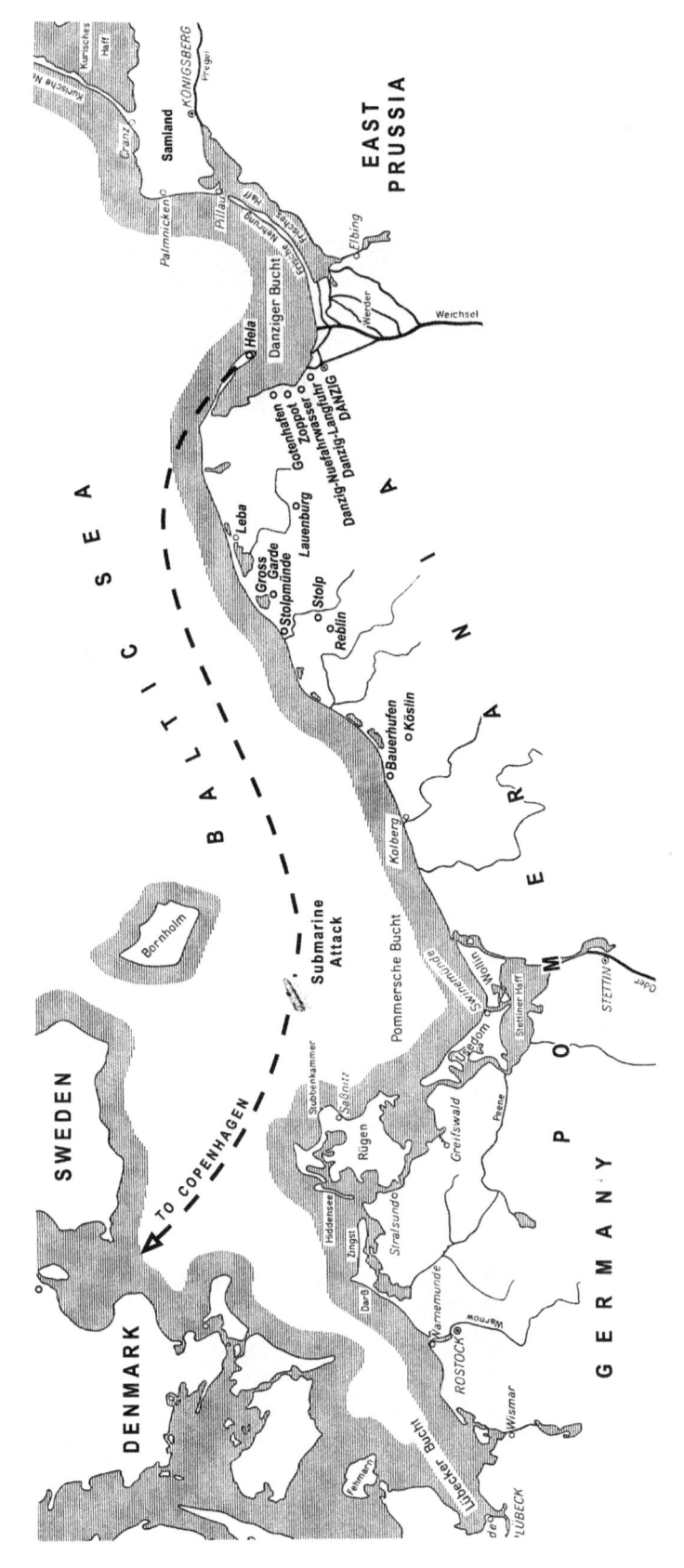

We invite you to view the complete
selection of titles we publish at:

www.TEACHServices.com

Scan with your mobile
device to go directly
to our website.

Please write or e-mail us your praises, reactions, or
thoughts about this or any other book we publish at:

P.O. Box 954
Ringgold, GA 30736

info@TEACHServices.com

TEACH Services, Inc., titles may be purchased in bulk for
educational, business, fund-raising, or sales promotional use.
For information, please e-mail:

BulkSales@TEACHServices.com

Finally, if you are interested in seeing
your own book in print, please contact us at

publishing@TEACHServices.com

We would be happy to review your manuscript for free.

www.ingramcontent.com/pod-product-compliance
Lightning Source LLC
Chambersburg PA
CBHW081925170426

43200CB00014B/2839